SPIT TEMPLE

THE SELECTED PERFORMANCES OF CECILIA VICUÑA

EDITED BY ROSA ALCALÁ

TABLE OF CONTENTS

Illapantac[1]

Al canto
se rompen

las aguas
del llanto

las que
media rán

cantá
rito
roto
la fer ti lidad

el canto
les abre

grueso portal
quiébralo dentro

que hay que llevar
el canto quebrado

que hay que comer

templo e'saliva
que no ha de volver

---

1. "Illapantac" and an earlier version of its translation appear in *cloud-net*. New York: Art in General, 1999. 62-63.

Illapantac

To song
the waters

of wailing
break

they will
mediate

                    pitch, a fertile
                    rite
                    a little
                    broken pitch
                    er

song
opens

a heavy portal
smash it in

it's time to de
cant, to begin

eating

the fractured
song

spit temple
to never return

INTRODUCTION

"Made Not of Words, But Forces": Cecilia Vicuña's Oral Performances

Rosa Alcalá

I.

JUST WHAT IS THIS WOMAN DOING?

Gathered with dozens of people in a small library at Brown University—too small, in fact, for the number who have shown up—I wait for the invited poet to approach the podium. There has been the usual introduction and applause, but after several minutes of silence, she is nowhere in sight. As I nervously scan the room looking for her, the silence gives way to the sound of audience members shifting uncomfortably in their seats. Then, at the height of tension, singing—a cluster of vowels, really—begins to rise up from somewhere among the rows of chairs, first quietly, then growing louder and more persistent, until it seemingly permeates even the library's polished wood. Cecilia Vicuña emerges suddenly from within the audience, having wrapped wool thread around those sitting next to her. Continuing her high-pitched chant, she slowly and deliberately approaches the podium, pulling the thread behind her. Relieved, I expect her, despite the unusual entrance, to introduce herself, say a few words, and begin reading from *Unravelling of Words & the Weaving of Water*, the book that prompted this event in progress. In fact, I organized this reading on the strength of her book, knowing little about her, and there are poems I am hoping she'll read, some favorites she might explain, into which she might offer insight. Still, she's not reading—at least not in the usual sense; instead, she sings, chants, whispers, navigates a registry of sounds, swiftly moving between languages (Spanish and English, perhaps others I don't recognize). With her voice and intonation she explores the musicality within words, changing their very meaning. Or she becomes quiet, compelling us to listen to the birds singing outside of the library, so that in the absence of her voice, we listen to what's present at the edges of the university. There are books and papers in front of her, but this is, without a doubt, not a "poetry reading" in the usual sense—an oral reproduction of text on the page framed by anecdotal remarks, performed with that "reading" voice so familiar to us all. And while I expect her to read poems written in Spanish, then equitably offer their English translation, her movement between languages is less than predictable. I keep listening for the poems that I remember, and maybe I recognize a phrase or an idea now and again, but so much of it, I think, must simply be poetry I have not yet read. I can't say for sure if what I have just experienced is a "poetry reading"; I only know I am sure that it is poetry.

This first experience of Vicuña's reading in 1995—confusing and appealing at once—perhaps resembles the experiences many audiences have had watching her performances, as Rodrigo Toscano confirms when he voices the audience's collective uneasiness by asking, "just what is this woman doing?"[1] But what does the audience expect "this woman"—this poet—to do? Where does the audience expect to be taken within the space of the poetry reading? In a very basic sense, the audience wants to witness a kind of authenticity, the poem read by the person who wrote it. But that place is also one that is enforced by determined parameters, known well by those in attendance: there is a poet at the podium, there's a poem on the page to be read, there's witty preamble to the poem, and an audience in its place holding its applause until the end. All of it followed by the polite sale of books. In other words, the place the audience expects to inhabit—at best a "transcendent" space where poems open up in an exchange between audience and poet—is always-already encoded and predetermined. These conventions remain in place despite a century of challenges to their primacy: Kurt Schwitter's phonetic experiments at the Cabaret Voltaire, The Four Horsemen's apocalyptic cacophonies, David Antin's "uninterrupted dialogues," or Augusto De Campos's "verbivocovisual" dimensions. In fact, there are many examples of poetry performance in the twentieth and twenty-first centuries that don't adhere to the conventional reading of poetry—and yet, what we normally expect from a poetry reading remains more or less intact.

Certainly, Vicuña's approach to the space of the reading challenges those of us schooled in the twentieth-century Anglo-American poetry reading tradition and its conventions, but perhaps what makes Vicuña's performances exceptional, and what challenges on a deeper level the poetry reading's primary convention—the reading of poems printed on a page—is not her unusual entrance or the use of thread, but the ways she re-imagines and animates the text by singing, improvising, and altering, in performance, her printed poems. In general, poetry readings—even when they are called performances—often reflect our general privileging of literacy over orality; despite poetry's origins in orality, we expect readings to be merely fleeting enactments of poems that properly exist in books. As a result, the printed versions of poems—as is true for most poets in the age of print—are seen as the quintessential archive through which we measure the poet's work and through which the poet is to measure herself. It's true that there exists no dearth of recordings of poets reading their poems, but these recordings, while perhaps bringing a poem "to life," rarely upset the centrality of the printed poem, and, more likely, reinforce it.

In addition to those oral performances which occur within the space of the poetry reading, Vicuña also delivers performance-lectures within the space of the conference or lecture hall. Here, Vicuña continues to challenge dominant paradigms by eschewing the usual formulas for argumentation or observation found in panel discussions and "talks." Vicuña's performative and less formal approach—"more ceremonial than academic," as Linda Duke describes the Krannert performance-lecture—is similar to her recent critical "poem-essays" on Emma Kunz ("The Melody of Structures") and Mayan dress ("Ubixic del decir"). Unlike most papers, which foreground an argument or thesis, building support through theoretical and textual evidence in a linear fashion toward a totalizing conclusion, the overlapping threads of her poem-essays and performance-lectures enact a flexible and multi-directional thinking-through of ideas. In a sense, she pushes the academic argument closer to that of poetry, and as with her poetry performances, Vicuña's "papers" would be difficult to reproduce in journals—because they are improvised rather than read, and, more important, because most journals would not recognize them as proper academic arguments.

If we consider Vicuña's work through this lens, the problem is that the oral performances—because they are rarely straight readings of papers or poems in books, and because they are improvised and ephemeral—rarely exist as print texts. Yet, one could easily argue that Vicuña's performances are, in many ways, her definitive works, and are at the very least key to understanding her work as a whole. Despite their importance, however, little has been written about them, and few recordings or transcriptions have been made available to the public. Most who have written on her work have discussed some element of her oral performances, or have looked at the ways in which the notion of performance (or the performative) intersects much of her work.[2] But few have studied extensively the oral performances themselves.[3] All that exists to document her extensive work in oral performance, therefore, are a few transcriptions and recordings on the Internet.[4]

Listening to Quasars

Although Vicuña is focused on oral performance, hers is no romantic idea of a pristine orality. It is one fully cognizant of the intervention of print, and is concerned mainly with the interplay between poetic texts and the vocalization and improvisation of those texts. This "spoken poetics," Sherwood writes, must be understood as "interface or hybrid (and not a 'transitional technique') between the oral and the written" (78). Echoing the darker side of historical debates concerning orality and textuality, Vicuña, instead, refers to the space between them as "a war zone" whose frontline is necessarily the performance (personal interview). In this "war zone" Vicuña weaves together improvised narratives with previously written or published poems she modifies in performance. This alteration of texts in performance is what Sherwood refers to as "versioning," meaning that Vicuña creates new, in situ, renderings of her poems by changing language or phrasing, or alters the standard edition by singing, whispering or chanting.[5] Poems are "versioned" between or as part of the improvised narratives, which in turn begin as notes handwritten with a certain site or concern in mind, sometimes days or hours before the performance. Compared to her published poems, neatly printed and bound in books, her notes appear to be disorganized, random compositions floating across the page, the detritus of transitory thoughts jotted on a small hotel notepad, each page torn as it is read. And unlike the poems which circulate in print, these notes are simply filed away after each performance, having fulfilled their function as a kind of score for the performance. While one might think of this technique as improvisation, a making new in the instant, Sherwood has us reconsider the limitations of "improvisation" as a description for Vicuña's performances, suggesting instead that we think of the technique as "more a kind of listening."[6] Sherwood suggests, in other words, that Vicuña isn't letting herself go in just any direction, as we might associate with improvisation, but instead is listening to and harnessing, in a purposeful way, the energies and memories of language itself. We might think of Jack Spicer's definition of a poet: one who is open to signals from the "outside," which he or she "receives" like a radio (or, less receptively, as a "counter-punching radio") and processes into poems.[7]

This listening, however, Sherwood points out, extends beyond the language of the poems and notes Vicuña transforms in performance, to the specificities of the performance space itself. By listening to the sounds and dimensions of her surroundings, she seems to welcome not only the unstable elements of the present moment as they intersect with her performance, but also acknowledges the site as its own "text," with its history, signs, movements. She may recognize, for instance, that Hallwalls Contemporary Art Center in Buffalo, NY, a space now dedicated to contemporary art, was once a factory, releasing "toxic gas."[8] Or she may allow ambient elements to merge with or unhinge the performance, rather than ignore them or block them out (as one would during most conventional poetry readings). In other words, she is drawing connections between what we think of as the discrete venue and the world of which the poetry speaks. In her 1995 performance at The Poetry Project at St. Mark's Church, for example, Vicuña relates the myth of the Pishtako, a monstrous being that is, in fact, "the sound / of all these machines / at work / in Lima... that's eating / and feeding / on the blood / and grease / and body / of all the Indians," then directs the audience's attention to the stream of New York street noise permeating the walls of the space. Sometimes the relationship between site and performance is much more contentious; as Jena Osman observes, "At Art in General, the ambient elements are like an insurgency. Just about everything that could disrupt our focus does so. The sound system isn't working correctly. The elevator door is tremendously noisy—like a garage door opening, accompanied by a game-show bell. The floors themselves are very 'responsive'—offering something back for each step they receive."[9] Yet, even in this case, Vicuña incorporates the disruptions into the performance.

Vicuña's "listening" leads not to the usual display of mastery but to performance as unstable and unpredictable event. It is through the performance that the idea or poem on paper becomes what Vicuña calls a "quasar," "an about to happen." Vicuña writes that her quasar looks "for a form before the form," adding, "A poem only becomes poetry when its structure / is made not of words but forces." The quasar is not a tangible thing—a poem or story to be told—but a process of discovery that allows the evolving elements of the performance to manifest. Vicuña has also referred to the quasars as "not-yet poems" or "quasi poems,"[10] which suggests that what manifests in these oral performances reveals threads that may later be pulled into the future design of a written poem. As a result, the poem sometimes moves from performance to page, rather than the conventional movement from page to performance. Peformance, in other words, provides the warp and weft upon which any text may—or may not—be woven; and at the same time in performance, all texts are subject to change, all are precarious and "about to happen," all are threads to be spun into a larger, continual textile, which is the interconnected worlds we inhabit.

A Thousand Tiny Fibers Dissolving In Air

This entanglement of the oral and the written "so that they are in tension like lovemaking" is, as Vicuña claims of indigenous Latin American textile, "what makes the weaving sacred." But the possibilities of that tension lie foremost in the "unspun wool"—the undeveloped elements of the performance. In her 1998 Hallwalls performance she says, "People say that / unspun wool / contains the power / of the cosmos / because it's not yet— / it's nothing you see / it has not been spun / it's no thing / it's pure potential." These threads of unspun wool, so omnipresent in her visual art, with their symbolic connection to the Latin American tradition of weaving, also play, thematically, a major role in the oral performances. The thread can become, metaphorically, a genetic line, one that overlaps and fuses with other genetic lines: "each one of our lines...continuing and completing the next." And in this merging of genes, voice becomes that which is composed of many other voices, the vocal chords imagined as a bundle of threads caught up in language's own knotty web. To speak a language, in other words, is to invoke multiple origins, the spun and unspun wool of cultural histories; it is to enact, as Walter Mignolo says, "the 'natural' plurilingual conditions of the human world 'artificially' suppressed by the monolingual ideology and monotopic hermeneutics of modernity and nationalism" (228). Vicuña's search for her own genetic makeup has been an attempt to upset such fictions; she discovered through a DNA test that her grandmother—despite her family's claim that "there was no indigenous ancestry" (Isbell 50)—probably had Diaguita blood. In her 1998 Barnard College performance, Vicuña tells us that these unacknowledged or actively suppressed threads in our perceived origins emerge in performance of the everyday, particularly in song. And we can hear them if only we listen. Tracing Spanish back to the Arabic, for instance, she describes the "melodic matrix" present in the vocal chords of the mother who, singing a lullaby to her child, voices "the migrations of words" / "the migration of sounds." Intuitive rather than learned or mastered, Vicuña's singing—what she calls "musical debris"—is thus an attempt to connect viscerally, as the mother does with the child, to a field of meaning vibrating beneath the surface of words, an unregulated, invisible and alternate knowledge.

This "melodic matrix" can also hold the "ancestral memory suppressed by official culture" that Vicuña first recognized in Violeta Parra's "dissonant" voice, a dissonance that helped recover Chile's forgotten folk songs and launch the New Chilean Song in the 1960s. Parra's work thus exemplifies Vicuña's insistence that despite the suppression or selectivity of lineages and histories evidenced by our atomized voices, it is what we choose to hear beneath or within our voices that can reveal the lost threads of suppressed wor(l)ds, and thus enact a change of perspective that might instigate a change in our social framework. Vicuña points out that the etymology of "tone" is a stretched thread, so that to refer to "tone of voice" is to understand speech as the weaving of "a thousand tiny fibers dissolving in air." But this dissolution does not absolve the speaker of responsibility to the lost threads of the world, as she says at the Woodland Pattern performance: "fate is to speak / and you fate yourself as you speak / as you name the name." She suggests that fate is, in fact, not predetermined, but is a weaving enacted by what and how we choose to speak or name. Thus, by naming what lies beneath the surface, to put oneself at risk by speaking rather than safely reciting without attention to the present, is to perform the aesthetic of ethical action on which so much of Vicuña's work depends.

In her 1998 Hallwalls performance, Vicuña arrives at the podium with a white thread woven between the fingers of her right hand. As she performs and gesticulates, the threads move in rhythm with the voice, seeming at times a deliberate punctuation of the accompanying performance. As she describes a thread installation envisioned in a dream, for instance, the dream seems to materialize between her hands. Then, when the dream becomes a reality, and she witnesses threads across La Plaza de Mayo in Buenos Aires, hung with the pictures of the disappeared, victims of the military regime, the tensioned thread suggests the connection between the conscious and the unconscious, between the living and the dead. Later, as she describes an old woman lost in travel who drinks from water gathered in depressions left in the dirt by animal hooves, Vicuña raises her cupped hand to her mouth, and the strings dangle like drops of water falling between her fingers. Even as her hand moves naturally, an involuntary accompaniment to her speaking, the thread becomes a conspicuous part of the narrative, a white peak that mimics the "geysers" coming out of holes in a Manhattan street. With this ephemeral book of gestures, Vicuña draws attention to the body's stitch, the way it threads the eyes of words; this ephemeral book of gestures traces, too, all those disappearances, those omissions, hemmed invisibly, violently, into the official versions of who and what we are.

This pulling at the threads of disappearances, then, that hold together our social fabric, our histories, is at the center of Vicuña's performances. In her 1995 Poetry Project performance, Vicuña tells us about the last Selk'nam woman shaman, Lola Kiepja, and the tragic events surrounding the disappearance of her people, and with them, a language and culture. Singing a lament for Kiepja, Vicuña's voice digs deep into the subterranean and subcutaneous layers of all losses. But disappearance can also mean "farmers / losing / crop / varieties / as / species / dwindle," Vicuña warns us during a 1999 performance at the Krannert Art Center, a reflection of her attention to ecological destruction, beginning in the 1960s and central to her work. Together, these accounts, like the photographs of the disappeared hanging over the Plaza de Mayo, string together and make visible a world of connection that either we can't see or choose not to notice, while leading us to an awareness of the possibilities and political implications of collectively following the thread. Furthermore, these performances, because they build their strength on instability, at the precipice of disappearance, become symbolic ground on which to trace such loss.

Even suppressed or discarded accounts, like official ones, are never static, they must be understood against changing contexts. It is interesting to note, then, how her narratives of disappearance change and adapt to different sites and historical moments, how they reveal differently at different times, and how they thread themselves in and out of performances. Take, for instance, Vicuña's invocation of Luis Gómez, a migrant worker from Ecuador, who, according to Somini Sengupta of the *New York Times*, was buried alive on July 10, 1998 near Vicuña's apartment in the Tribeca section of Manhattan, while working for Safeway Construction, a company contracted by Con Edison. In the notes for the 1998 Hallwalls performance, we find several lines dedicated to Gómez, and in performance these lines become a burial rite, a lament for the disappeared immigrant. Vicuña develops her narrative from six lines in the right hand column of her notes, but omits from the actual performance several more lines beneath them, which say: "some time ago / writing / about one of those / doors, / a few meters away / I said: / writing is the door / of the under / world // the body / of those who / disappear / in the / writing." Three years later, only days after the events of September 11, 2001, Vicuña once again re-tells this neighborhood story or *New York Times* report, exhuming, then re-animating, the memory of the buried worker. This time, however, in her performance at Woodland Pattern Book Center, September 29, 2001, the loss of one life comes to represent that of many. Vicuña, who since 1980 has lived just a few blocks from where the World Trade Center once stood, was greatly impacted by the events of Sept. 11—not only did dust and debris infiltrate her apartment and studio, but the devastation brought her back to the despair and helplessness she felt while living in London and learning of the Chilean military coup of 1973, which also occurred on September 11. During the performance, Vicuña begins by making reference to the *cloud-net* performance[11] filmed by the Hudson River in 1998 only blocks from the World Trade Center, and then says simply, "The towers disappeared and they became this white light going up…" Vicuña then proceeds with a version of the Luis Gómez story, and in doing so, emphasizes the importance of remembering, among the larger tragedies, those individual losses that often go undocumented or unnoticed, those bodies that "disappear in the writing." Sometime between the 1998 performance at Hallwalls and the 2001 performance at Woodland Pattern, then, emerges a poem about Luis Gómez, appearing in the journal *Cross Cultural Poetics* in 2001. The poem is distinct from but shares elements with these performances; it is hard to know whether Vicuña transformed the already written poem in performance, or whether the poem came later, as a result of the performed narrative.

Some of the "unspun wool" for the narratives that ground the oral performances are culled from recent events, "web gossip" (as we see in Vicuña's telling of Cacique Guaicaipuro Cuatemoc's address to the European Union at the Poetry Project at St. Mark's Church, 2002), current news of scientific discoveries, pop culture, history, and everyday observations. With the help of her performance notes, they are pulled out of the mundane, anecdotal, or disposable, and into the field of myth-making, as Sherwood has pointed out. Maria Damon sees the emphasis of myth in Vicuña's performances as an affirmation of its basic human function: "A creation myth is recreated every day, out of the everyday matter of breath and cloth, eating, sleeping, speaking, breathing."[12] If we now consider the Internet, the World Wide Web, as a form of the basic human communicative function (one, not coincidentally, modeled on weaving), Vicuña reminds us at her 1999 Krannert performance that our ethical use of these materials, our "weaving" of them, depends on the "we we we" suggested by the acronym for the World Wide Web.

Where Borders Shift

The oracular quality of the performances has a great deal to do with the way in which Vicuña performs these narrative and versioned poems. It is as if they were part of an ongoing oral epic yet to be written down ("the storyteller continuing the parable," Edwin Torres writes), the intimacy of her half-whispering but insistent voice imparting cohesion to the various elements. As both Torres and Dennis Tedlock mention, this voice, without adjusting volume, navigates a range of pitches and tones, suggesting that when Vicuña repeatedly asks if she can be heard, she's not asking whether she needs to speak more loudly or adjust the microphone.[13] Instead, she is asking those in the audience to adjust their hearing, to lean forward, to listen along with her. The poems, the venue, the audience, the narratives, and the disappeared threads of the world, all become connected in that distinctive voice, rather than delimited by category or function: "poem," "anecdote," "joke," "song," "ambient noise, "gestures," or "observation." All elements, through Vicuña's performative voice, are pulled into this elusive, emergent event she calls the quasar.

She does this by allowing few or no boundaries between the elements—pauses or shifts that would indicate the transition between, say, a preamble and a poem. If we consider the reading of poems as discrete events that are bracketed off from the larger event of the poetry reading by means of introductions—where the poet gives the poem's background, for example, or simply announces the start of a new poem by giving the title—then Vicuña rarely employs what Erving Goffman refers to as an "episoding convention."[14] Vicuña's narratives are not explanations that precede the reading of a poem. Because she rarely pauses to emphasize the title of a poem, and sometimes omits it altogether, it is in fact easy to miss the transition from narrative or commentary to a versioned poem—none of these elements is framed as such. As Sherwood has argued, Vicuña's lack of hesitation between these elements suggests not only "interrelated forms," but a new version of the poem itself, connected to the evolving oral performance ("Sound Written" 88), and perhaps, therefore, even a new version of poetry.

In performance, Vicuña's "high, wispy Andean voice" (Lippard 14) similarly works its way indiscriminately through both English and Spanish, incorporating words and concepts found in languages indigenous to Latin America (Quechua, Mapuche, others), and lets them ride together, occasionally working in an explanation or translation. Vicuña traces this mix of languages to the late 80s, when she found herself without a translator and was forced to "improvise in a mixture of English, Quechua, and Spanish." In turn, this multilingual improvisation, Vicuña claims, caused "the borders between the written and the oral [...] to shift."[15] Because since 1980 Vicuña's performances have been largely for English-speaking audiences in the United States, these language shifts—this English made non-standard in the mouth of a native Spanish speaker, this Spanish in a mostly non-Spanish setting—create different levels of opacity and unintelligibility, depending on the listener. In crossing, with and without papers, the language borders maintained by most social structures (even that of the poetry reading), Vicuña performs what Walter Mignolo calls "languaging": a "thinking and writing between languages, that moves us away from the idea that language is a fact (e.g., a system of syntactic, semantic, and phonetic rules), and [moves us] toward the idea that speech and writing are strategies for orienting and manipulating social domains of interaction" (226). In her printed poems, a similar thing occurs; as Vicuña examines their origins or fuses different languages, words move through and open up new and forgotten histories and meanings. As Hugo Méndez-Ramírez explains, "Once we go beyond the surface of words and enter their etymologies, we discover that the languages and cosmogonies of many cultures are intertwined" (66). For Vicuña, words are not just the inheritors of tradition, but can perform outside of their conscripted roles, if we let them. In her poems, verbs might dress up like nouns, a noun might move like a verb, migrating into uncharted territory, mating (or merely flirting) with what and whomever it chooses.

Hazards & Holes

While they are different in emphasis (one on the oral and the other on the visual, even though these two categories sometimes overlap), there are a number of similarities between Vicuña's oral performances—which exist in that "war zone" between voice and text—and her performance and visual art, which could be said to exist in the "war zone" between object and ritual. Taking cues from performance and conceptual art—including both land art and installation—Vicuña's more visual performances signify (often symbolically) through the arrangement and movement of objects and bodies, and create, as her oral performances also often do, a ritual space. Many of these performances have served to protest political, social, or ecological injustice—from the much-discussed 1979 Vaso de leche (Glass of Milk) street performance in Bogotá, Colombia,[16] to a recently filmed performance at the Nevado del Plomo in Chile, where Vicuña extended on the ground blood-red strands of wool, several feet long, arranging them like streams flowing down the mountain, and sat at the end of one strand, holding it between her splayed legs to resemble menstrual blood. This un-announced mountaintop performance preceded a street performance in front of Palacio La Moneda, Chile's government palace (the Centro Cultural, just under the palace, was the site where Vicuña had installed "El Quipu Menstrual" as part of the 2006 group show, "The Other Side: Chilean Women Artists"). The street performance involved several participants carrying a similar blood-red strand, but several inches thicker in diameter, from the policed doors of La Moneda to a fountain, where they immersed it in water. The performances and installation were meant as a protest against the Chilean government's approval of the gold-mining project Pascua-Lama, initiated by the Barrick Gold Corporation of Canada, which would allow the company, according to local environmental and civic groups, "to harm the local water supply, destroy agriculture, and walk away without paying taxes or royalties" (Rohter). Although Vicuña, in general, is not recognized as part of the surge of performance art in Latin America during the 1960s and 1970s, her visual, as well as oral, performance, in its political intent and invocation of ritual, might therefore usefully be considered within the context of much of the work discussed in Coco Fusco's anthology, *Corpus Delecti: Performance Art of the Americas*.[17]

Vicuña's "quasars" are also properly understood within the context of two other major manifestations of her own visual art, the *precarios* and the large-scale, in situ thread installations like *cloud-net*. The *precarios* or precarious objects—which Vicuña also refers to as basuritas or "little litter"—are small, fragile objects composed of man-made and natural refuse (twigs, roots, pencils, a plastic grid) that are "installed" like altars or offerings in urban or rural settings, and are therefore vulnerable to ocean tides, waves of pedestrians, and river currents. The in situ installations of the *precarios* are often unannounced, ephemeral performances to which no audience is invited or expected. At other times, these objects are displayed as sculptures in a gallery, assembled and disassembled for each exhibition. While both the in situ installations and the gallery displays of the *precarios* have often been photographed, their delicate nature makes these objects, as their name suggests, subject to time and the elements; they are prone to disintegration, and to a shifting of their composition, not unlike the unscripted and ephemeral quasars. Yet, the tensions between determinacy and indeterminacy, contingency and the absolute—so at the center of discussions regarding mid-century avant-garde practice—seem for Vicuña rather to be found more specifically in the ancient roots that underlie the notion of "the precarious," as she explains: "Precarious is what is obtained by prayer. Uncertain, exposed to hazards, insecure. From the Latin 'precarious,' from 'precis; prayer'" (Precario 2).

Like the *precarios*, the large-scale thread installations have been part of her work since the early part of her career. These installations respond to the architectural specificities of a room and the conventions of an institution, restructuring its navigable space by extending unspun wool across it, like a web or net. And like so much of her work, the thread installations recall the indigenous Latin American traditions of weaving, as well as the pre-Columbian mnemonic devices made of knotted thread known as quipus, which require the fingers, rather than the eyes, to read what it records. By putting into dialogue modernist art practice with the indigenous, as other Latin American artists and writers had done before her, she simultaneously recovers the "ancestral memory suppressed by official culture" and gestures towards movements such as surrealism and dadaism, which she claims as early influences. In doing so, Vicuña has consistently drawn from the rich cultural reserves of Latin American thought and art, as well as its pre-Columbian legacy, much like the body-centered performance artists featured in Fusco's book. This attention to the local, Fusco reminds us, is in contrast to European modernists who sought the "new" outside of their native Europe (7-8). Vicuña's art work, then, like Latin America's own mestizaje, reflects both the difficult and generative marriage of indigenous and European cultural production. But more than simply sites of syncretism, the installations, too, refer to the erasure or undervaluation of indigenous cultures. We see a poignant example of this in "A Net of Holes," an installation of a grid or net made from black yarn, sagging from the corner of a ceiling at the 1997 Whitney Biennial. This installation—which often went unnoticed by visitors unless a museum guard stationed beneath it prompted them to look up—was, according to Vicuña, "a statement of invisibility" meant to echo an anonymous Nahuatl poem relating the Spanish conquest of Tenochtitlan, the Aztec capital, which says, "Our only legacy was a net of holes /but not even shields can /hold such emptiness."[18] But "A Net of Holes," can also be understood as a statement of hope and possibility, as the installation, according to Vicuña, invokes another voice, that of modern Cuban poet, José Lezama Lima, who writes: "El vacío es calmoso / lo podemos atraer con un hilo"[19] (qtd in Martin 68).

Vicuña's artistic formation was also decidedly influenced by the non-objective avant-garde tendencies of the 1960s and 70s—a time when body art, happenings, and groups like Fluxus or Arte Povera were questioning the commodification of the art object, favoring instead process-oriented and participatory art. In Latin America specifically, performances or "actions" during this time were simultaneously responding to the "disappearance of bodies, the brutality of the military and the police, the censuring of contestatory voices, and open warfare against political opposition" by "infus[ing] avant-garde strategies with social and political orientations, to address state institutions, and to envision the deployment of art in public space as a symbolic confrontation with the state" (Fusco 9). From the beginning, influenced as she was by the potential she saw in Salvador Allende's socialist Popular Unity government, Vicuña understood art as a form of political engagement. While in Chile during the late 60s and early 1970s, Vicuña produced, in addition to paintings and poems, conceptual art and installations—such as a gallery filled with leaves, which she offered as homage to socialism[20]. With the Tribu No, a group of friends and artistic collaborators, Vicuña performed her poems and participated in actions, interrupting, for example, the International Writers Conference held in Chile in 1969, to which the group had not been invited. There they distributed among the literary and government dignitaries handwritten fliers that combined quotes from well-known writers, such as Antonin Artaud, with those penned by Tribu No, denouncing "functionaries who drink cocktails with government ministers," and declaring, "Long live poetry," "Long live the displaced."

In London, where she arrived in 1972 on scholarship to the Slade School of Fine Arts, Vicuña began to create a "Diary of Objects"—a collection of *precarios*—by picking up and arranging street debris. Simultaneously, Vicuña began *Saboramí*, a book documenting and incorporating some of these objects. But as the threat of the military coup grew closer, the tone and message of the book changed, and she began to incorporate poems, journal entries, and explicit denunciations of both the Chilean military and U.S. involvement in the coup. It was while assembling *Saborami* on a farm in Devon, England (the site of Beau Geste Press, the book's publisher) that news of events surrounding the Chilean military coup began to reach Vicuña. As a result, *Saborami,* with its scatterings of found objects and writings, became an aesthetic representation of the fragmentation and loss that had begun to manifest in the country from which she was now estranged—a representation of her own sense of helplessness and resulting exile. In his introduction to *Saborami*, Felipe Ehrenberg, artist and co-editor of *Beau Geste*, writes,

> Appearing as it does two months after Chile was carefully raped by starry striped militarists, *Saborami* is the very first howl of pain to emerge from the rubble under which Chile's conscience lies stunned. This book is sheer irony; the result of converging chance happenings: it collects nearly ten years of work by Cecilia and was planned as a celebration. Now it symbolizes the contained fury and the sorrow of her country's present. It also gives an inkling of the strengths that will fight to break the New Disorder now in power.

Years later, discussing the fused particles of languages in her book *Instan*, Vicuña points back to the Chilean military coup, claiming, "after that moment I have lived mostly in english. the coup disintegrated language...the disintegration of my speech began when that axe blow was inflicted on us. if we are to be made into litter and cast-offs, then fine, I assume that position, I am garbage and a cast-off, and that is my language, the exploded fragment" (E-mail to the author). And in assuming this position in her performances as well, she allows one to hear an "inkling of the strengths" that can come as Vicuña gathers, from bits of poems and hints of notes, through songs and whispers, the threads of disappeared languages, lives, cultures, and histories, to weave a larger, collaborative, and ever-changing whole. It is thus through listening with these performances that one hears how the ephemeral, the seemingly fragile, can stand up against, and even topple, that which profits through such disappearances.

II.

WITH A LITTLE SPIT

The title of this book, *Spit Temple*, is derived from my translation of a poem Vicuña wrote and published in the catalog for her *cloud-net* exhibition. "Illapantac," the poem's title, and the word contained in it, "Illapa," refers to "the oldest deity in Andean myth," whose name "condenses thunder, lightning, and thunderbolt," and is therefore known to control "fluidity and rain." This deity is also the "supreme mediator of sound," and can go by the name "Pachacuti, 'world reverser'" (Vicuña, *cloud-net* 95). The poem—here in a new translation—describes the fertile and transformative powers of song, which can break open the vessel of creation, launching a series of changes from which there is no return. This poem condenses then, too, Vicuña's own poetics: to sing the text, to break it open, to unpack and mediate what is found there, is to open up a space for possibility. It is to create something that cannot be repeated. As Heather McHugh reminds us, *poeisis*, poetry's Greek root, means "to make," but the poem itself is a construct that differentiates itself formally from other writing by means of breaking itself into lines and stanzas (278). Moreover, a poem quilts itself from pieces or fragments of language, ideas, experiences, etc., and unifies or places them within the frame of the poem. In this sense, Vicuña's oral performances—these quasars—heighten the poetic process by reveling in a circular act of mending and fracturing, of moving in and out of frame.

Pulled from the translation of "Illapantac," the phrase "spit temple" is, first, meant to emphasize the centrality of the body in Vicuña's work, exploring its dangers and vulnerabilities, but also its sacredness. This is evident in conceptual projects from the late 60s and early 70s, particularly her "Dictionary of Come-ons and Insults," and "'Museums of Hair and Fingernails' in shoeboxes" (Vicuña, *The Precarious / Quipoem* q33), as well as her painting, "Manraja, menstruating angel" (1973), with its naked girl sitting on a tree, legs spread open and eyes rolled back as if in agony or ecstasy. However, it is also meant to reflect the ways in which Vicuña's oral performances challenge not only the sanctity of the "poetry reading," but also that of the printed text, consecrating and desecrating them equally, as a means to explore the borders between them.

Central to this exploration is Vicuña's notion of the precarious, which suggests that to venerate the text, to pray to and for it, is to "expose [it] to hazards." This tension between danger and possibility inherent in the precarious gestures towards Mary Douglas's claim that "[s]acred rules are thus merely rules hedging divinity off, and uncleanness is the two-way danger of contact with the divinity" (9). The linguistic paradox, Douglas points out, is at the very root of sacred, the Latin "sacer," which "has this meaning of restriction through pertaining to the gods. And in some cases may apply to desecration as well as to consecration" (10). According to Douglas, this "hedging off" or demarcation of what is sacred and profane, varying from culture to culture, can also be located in the body, which like all structures, is most "dangerous" and "vulnerable" at its margins—its orifices, tear ducts, and pores (150). In performance, the text—clean, contained, solid on the page—becomes contaminated by the voice of the performer, spit and air mixing to form words that then "dissolve in the air" and come in contact with and enter the listener.

Spit Temple is divided into four sections. The first is "Performing Memory: An Autobiography," written by Vicuña in Spanish specifically for this book, and translated here. Grounding her aesthetic in an historical and lived context, Vicuna's performative re-telling of her life is accompanied by photographs from her archives, many of which have never before been reproduced. The next section, "Poetics of Performance," is comprised of two poems, "Quasar" and "K'isa Alango," that together trace Vicuña's approach to performance. The third and central section, "The Quasars: Selected Oral Performances (1995-2003)," includes transcriptions of several of Vicuna's performances, as well as performance notes. The final section, "Listening: Responses to Vicuña's Oral Performances," is a collection of short essays by Dennis Tedlock, Jena Osman, Linda Duke, Kenneth Sherwood, Juliana Spahr, Rodrigo Toscano, Edwin Torres, and Nada Gordon.

The oral performances transcribed in the third section fall into two categories. First are the poetry performances, which occur within the frame of the poetry reading and are composed of improvised narratives and versioned poems. These comprise most of the transcriptions. Second are the performance-lectures mentioned above, specifically those at Barnard College (1996) and the Krannert Art Center (1999), which occur within the frame of the academic conference. The origins of the performance-lecture can be traced perhaps to London, where, as a student in the 1970s, Vicuña was asked to give lectures about the arts in Chile, and about Chilean social democracy. While it is difficult to know to what extent Vicuña transgressed norms in her delivery, a twelve-page script of a talk from that time reflects an idealistic belief in social transformation through popular art that would set the stage for her oral performances. Discussing Chile's El Teatro Nuevo Popular, for example, she writes:

> [W]e have a piece about events happening during the nationalization of a textile industry. We go to the industry and rehearse in front of the workers asking them to participate. We perform a scene and we stop and ask: "How did things really happen?" "What changes do you propose?" In the beginning people are shy and reluctant to talk, but as we continue to work they become more and more involved and in the end they change completely our text, and the piece continues to change through rehearsals and also after we perform it in different places (Lecture on the Arts in Chile after 1970, Center for Contemporary Arts, London, 1973).

In Vicuña's description of the collaborative and improvisational process of the ambulatory Teatro Nuevo Popular, we get a glimpse of what's to come in her work—a mindfulness of place and presence in performance that often alters, in the instant, the spoken work. Similarly, the belief that poetry is not just written or spoken, but always becoming something else or bringing something else into being, is at the heart of her discussion of "the other poetry" (oral, improvised, popular, and anonymous): "I think 'the other poetry' is fertilizing Chilean Poetry. From this fermentation something is coming out, but none of this poetry is translated into English. Some of it has not been even published yet" ("Lecture" 4). It is conceivable—although impossible to know—that Vicuña deviated from the dense and lengthy script, particularly in the sections titled "Stories," and "Short Stories," in which she describes, for example, Chile's "magical island," Chiloe (8), and the ways in which people there avoid the work of sorcerers: getting a fat woman to urinate in the middle of the kitchen, putting twelve mounds of sand on the table to keep the devil occupied, having a communal exorcism by burning excrement (10). Such mythical and magical narratives seem like early versions of those that occur in the oral performances.

The idea to transcribe these oral performances was influenced by the work of Dennis Tedlock, Jerome Rothenberg, and others associated with the ethnopoetics movement, who broke new ground with their studies, transcriptions, and enactments of indigenous orality and performance, as well as by Kenneth Sherwood, who remains one of the few to write extensively about Vicuña's oral performances.[21] Borrowing methods developed by these scholars, the transcriptions here attempt a graphic representation of Vicuña's shifts in register and pauses by means of spacing, fonts, and size of type in order to capture not just what the words say, but how they are being said. In this graphic representation of register, I do not differentiate between the spoken languages; this isn't meant to erase their difference, but to suggest fluidity of movement between them, and to avoid the mark of otherness often suggested by italics or quotation marks. In this, I take my cues from Vicuña's own undifferentiated fusing of languages in her book *Instan*, which in turn takes cues from her own multilingual performances. Still, no transcription can capture the greatest marker of difference here, Vicuña's voice, with its pronunciations and accents, how it changes when moving from English to Spanish, how it inscribes the voice of the Chilean Spanish speaker on to the English. Vicuña's voice—every voice, really—embodies the threads of difference in a way impossible to achieve with standard, written languages, including the transcriptions included here. Thus, these transcriptions enact, too, a precarious and imperfect performance that can never become the definitive archive.

Locating performances to transcribe for this book required wading through several shelves of videotapes, cassettes, and discs in a dusty back closet of Vicuña's studio, where she kept recordings given to her by the universities, bookstores, or galleries that had hosted her performances, then attempting to find recordings that had decipherable audio or from which stills could be extracted. Transcriptions created from visual recordings include descriptions of what could be seen as well as heard; those relying on audio capture only what could be heard. Some of the performances here, however, were used despite their poor audibility. This can be seen in the performance for the opening of her *cloud-net* exhibition at Art in General (New York, 1999), where the conditions of the venue prevented an audible recording, and as a result, a complete transcription. Here I decided to capture what could be heard in the first few minutes of Vicuña's performance, between the creaking of the floor and the opening of the elevator doors, reflecting, as Jena Osman points out, the very difficulty of hearing the performance that night, its disruptions. Osman's essay, however, goes far to relate the fuller effect of the performance's dimensions, beyond what can be heard or seen on the videotape. Whereas some performances had poor audio or shaky camera work, two included here, at the Rarig Center and Pierogi Gallery, were never recorded. In order to re-animate these performances, I coupled Vicuña's notes with Maria Damon's and Rodrigo Toscano's recollections.

Finally, the short essays that form the last section of this book were solicited from poets and critics who had attended one or more of Vicuña's poetry performances. Because much of what can be understood of these performances takes place as they are being voiced, the aim is for the essays to provide greater insight into Vicuña's work by relating the experience of being there. Most of the contributors—Osman, Spahr, Toscano, Damon, Duke, Tedlock—wrote in response to a performance they had attended and which is included in this book, either in the form of transcription or performance notes. These contributors were aided by recordings, transcriptions, or copies of performance notes I provided for them, but as their essays show, they relied on a combination of memory and documentation, providing a re-reading of the event, keyed by some lingering effect /impression it had on them. Edwin Torres's essay, however, gives us an overview of the accumulative impact of Vicuña's performance style, then relates an experience altogether different from that of the public performance—a much more intimate one—of recording her in a small apartment, with sound equipment in a closet, for an issue of *Rattapallax*. Accompanied by an essay, Kenneth Sherwood provides his own transcription of a performance, which, contrasted against the other transcriptions presented here, makes evident not only the individuality of listening, but also the possibilities for its graphic representation. Nada Gordon's essay, the last in the book, begins with notes she took during a performance at NYU in which Vicuña projected poem-drawings from her book *Instan*, and then proceeds to describe the connection between Vicuña's poetics and the book's contents.

To end *Spit Temple* with Gordon's essay on Vicuña's book *Instan* is to show the congregate influence that her evolving approach to performance has had on her written work. In *Instan*, the laboratory of corporeal movements found in her oral performances presents itself in two forms—visual poems and multilingual poems. *Instan*'s first section, "Gramma Kellcani (the drawings)"—derived from the "Greek gramma, to scratch, draw and write," and the Quechua verb meaning to write and draw" (notes, *Instan*)—contains a constellation of word-objects handwritten in pencil that look strikingly similar to her performance notes. The drawings spiral across or down the page, forming threads of genetic material, hovering at the margins: words as stars or spermatozoa, grids of multiple meanings, cells or chemical compositions. The last page features dots floating on a page, like decomposing letters, or far away planets, even quasars dictating poems. The incredibly subtle reproduction of this first section of *Instan*, in fact, tempts the reader to run a finger against the page to see if the penciled poem-drawings rub off, as if Vicuña had just written them. The sections that follow the visual poems, "el poema cognado / the poem" and "fábulas del comienzo y restos del origen / fables of the beginning and remains of the origin," appear to provide a reading of the handwriting, a rendering of the histories beneath or traversing the word-objects. To say that this book feels informed by Vicuña's evolving poetics of performance is not to suggest that *Instan* represents a preferred direction or movement—from performance to print—since, as we have seen, all of Vicuña's texts loop back to performance, and some of the performance can sometimes become text. Rather, it suggests that in her work one cannot exist without the other.

The process of documenting Vicuña's oral performances, by bringing together these "lost" materials and people to comment on them, employs the dialectical or dialogic strategy Damon notes in Vicuña's work, one not looking for resolutions, but the constant tug and pull of opposing and mutable forces. By giving others a thread, as Vicuña does when she enters a performance, I was asking them to undo or reweave the experience in order that together we'd make something new, a quasar perhaps. These transcriptions and accompanying sections, therefore, are not the final say on Vicuña's oral performances; these performances are voiced now as they, borrowing Damon's words, "oscillate" or "merge," then "separate" and merge again with each reader who, bringing their own "Spit Temple," enters this "closed but permeable space."

III.

ACKNOWLEDGMENTS

The idea for *Spit Temple* began several years ago, in conversation with Darren Wershler-Henry, and along the way, many others have helped make that initial conversation into the book you are now holding.

I am grateful to the State University of New York at Buffalo, especially Professor Dennis Tedlock (McNulty Chair), for making it possible to conduct early research. It was in graduate seminars conducted by Tedlock, Charles Bernstein, and Shaun Irlam that the ideas contained here began to take shape. I am also grateful to the University of Texas at El Paso, where this book was completed.

Jeff Sirkin's careful and precise reading and editing of the manuscript is testament to his vast reserve of knowledge and patience. His belief in this project and in everything I do allowed me to continue despite numerous obstacles.

Kristin Dykstra, Roberto Tejada, and Kenneth Sherwood, with their generous and encouraging advice and commentary, gave me the final push to complete this book.

I'd also like to thank all of the contributors included here, who were quick to produce interesting and original essays, and who waited patiently for the book to materialize. A special thanks to Ugly Duckling Presse, especially Anna Moschovakis, for making beautiful and relevant books, and for taking time and care with this one.

And, finally, to Cecilia Vicuña, for putting her life in my hands—in the form of documents, tapes, photographs, conversations, and time. She allowed me to rummage through her house, and to keep irreplaceable archives for several years (and in two states). I hope this book repays her trust.

Despite everyone's generous contributions to *Spit Temple,* I accept all responsibility for its errors.

SPIT TEMPLE

THE SELECTED PERFORMANCES OF CECILIA VICUÑA

PERFORMING MEMORY: AN AUTOBIOGRAPHY

CECILIA VICUÑA
Translated by Rosa Alcalá

Chile: 1948-1972
London, England: 1972-1975
Bogotá, Colombia: 1975-1980
New York: 1980-2002

The Streams of Bellavista

Valle del Maipo, 1948

I was born in a space of silence, at the foot of a blue and eternal wall: the Andes Mountains. We lived in La Florida, surrounded by orchards and gardens, irrigation canals and crops. In Mapuche, *Maipo* or *maipun* means to plough or cultivate land.

I played with water and its reflections. I spoke to and hummed with the water's utterances, bathing twigs and dolls in its stream. At night, the toads croaked and the entire valley resonated with the now extinct *sapitos de cuatro ojos* orchestra.

My mother played lullabies on her guitar, singing in an invented Mapuche:
"Amo tu anay, amo tu anay..."

My father taught me to speak by reciting Rubén Darío:
"Margarita está linda la mar y el viento lleva esencia sutil de azahar..."

There was no TV, only my mother's 8 mm home movies.

La Niña Atahuallpa, or Hen Girl
Bellavista, 1952

My first boyfriend was a rooster. At all hours, he watched over me. Perhaps thinking I was a hen.

Performance with Airplanes
Valle del Maipo, 1952

We lived far from Santiago. Bored, my mother would stage little theatrical productions in the garden.

She dressed my brother and me in ballet costumes to perform *Swan Lake,* with neither lake nor swan. My brother would appear among the weeds, looking for his love in the distance. I would emerge from between pink carnations, executing a *pas de bourrée* along the dirt path. Suddenly, a plane overhead would distract me, and I'd forget about the ballet. Camera in hand, my mother filmed all of it, only to later torture guests.

To Make a Mark Is to Tread on New Ground
Los Lilenes, 1952

On the beach I watched seagulls, their prints in the sand more beautiful than ours.

I played by making tracks in wet sand, avoiding the footprints of people I didn't like. I later learned it was better to walk on fresh sand.

Speaking to the Signs
Bellavista, 1952

My mother recounts the day she found me "writing." No one had taught me how to write. "What are you doing, *mijita*?" she asked. "I'm painting," I told her, and went on speaking to the signs.

Mouse Performance in the Teatro del Liceo Barros Arana
Santiago, 1953

My mother took me frequently to the ballet at Santiago's Municipal Theatre. I wanted to be a ballerina.

When I was four, she enrolled me in the Ballet Academy of Carlos Zadenyi, a Hungarian émigré. The company toured throughout the country, including Santiago's neighborhoods and schools. At five years old, my first role was that of a mouse in Ibsen's *A Doll's House*.

I was to fall to the ground, lift one leg, and play with my long, grey tail. I remember the feeling of being on stage: complete liberation! No longer the character "Cecilia," I was free to observe the audience. They became the spectacle, not me.

Ground Antenna
Santiago, 1954

My father built a trapeze in the patio. Hanging upside down, my brother and I became acrobats, specialists in an inverted worldview.

The Multilingual House
Santiago, 1950s

My parents dabbled in various tongues, and our house was filled with books in many languages: *The Divine Comedy* in Italian, art history in French, poetry in Portuguese. No one told me they were written in "other languages." I read and semi-understood them. Not understanding opened the door to other forms of imagining.

My brother and I played at speaking invented tongues, believing others would see us as "foreigners" who spoke "English."

Training in Fearlessness
Santiago, 1957

Without warning, we moved to the city, to a ritzy neighborhood where the kids made fun of me. They laughed because I danced my way to school, practicing moves that in dreams allowed me to fly. Or because I danced in my mother's movies. Or because instead of a school uniform, she'd send me off dressed as a flamenco dancer. And I spoke strangely, pronouncing words differently than the others. The teachers would ask, "And where are you from, dear?"

So I had to invent a way to overcome my fear:
—When kids threw rocks at me, I imagined that I wasn't a few feet away, but high above, among the galaxies, watching us on that tiny planet below.
—I was afraid of going blind, so I healed my fear by rehearsing blindness. I rode my bicycle with my eyes closed, trying to guide myself by sensing the irregularities of the pavement beneath the tires, like reading Braille.

We then moved downtown:
Elevators scared me, so I climbed the flat roofs of the highest buildings, and challenged the other children to run along the edge of the chasm.

The First Exile
Santiago, 1957

My first exile was leaving the countryside for the city, to enter San Gabriel, an Anglican school where they'd put Gringo soap[2] in the mouths of children who didn't speak English. And I didn't know a word of English! I began to learn through osmosis and sound, reciting "twinkle twinkle little star." I had never heard such a perfect word. "Twinkle" sounded exactly like a star performing—the shining of a sound.

2. Jabón Gringo was a brand of Chilean bar soap.

The Conversationalists
San Gabriel School, 1960

One day I suggested to my desk mate that we change the world. "How?" he asked. By talking, I told him. "But how can a conversation change the world?" "Two and two are four and four and two are six," I said. "All of humanity came from two people. If one person convinces another that injustice is unnecessary, that person will convince someone else, and so on." "Oh!" he said, and we started to talk to everyone. Shortly thereafter, I told a cousin about this plan, and she said, unimpressed, "But that's socialism!"

My Father's Library
1960-62

My grandfather, Carlos Vicuña Fuentes, was a writer and civil rights lawyer. In the 1940s he defended Pablo Neruda during the time of his persecution.[3] Our house was filled with poetry books, by Neruda, Vicente Huidobro, and Federico García Lorca. When I "discovered" Neruda, I imagined a stream of water running through his poems. Reading him was like drinking water from springs. But Huidobro had the most impact. Reading *Altazor* at twelve years old was like flying. Like lucid dreaming. There were no limits to his poetry.

3. Vicuña writes about this period in "Carta a los Bosques Pellümawida," published in *Rattapallax 11* (2004): "Deposed and hounded by the González Videla government, Neruda fled into clandestinity. My grandfather, Carlos Vicuña Fuentes, defended him, and the political police, thinking that we had him hidden, came to look for him at our house in the mountains. I was in my mother's womb, or hanging from a breast, newborn (I don't know). My grandfather says, 'Neruda is not here' and my aunt Lola intervenes, amusing herself: 'I know where Neruda is!' All are left speechless (even my grandfather): Where? 'Here,' she says mischievously, showing us a cartoon in *Topaze* magazine."

Góngora and Garcilaso

Liceo Manuel de Salas, Santiago, 1964

In high school we studied poetry from Spain's Golden Age by Góngora and Garcilaso. The kids hated it. No one could understand anything. The teacher would read a poem out loud and ask: "What does it mean?" No one dared to answer, but I stood up and offered an interpretation based on what I couldn't understand. After hearing me, the teacher said, "But you are creating a new poem." Inside of those poems, I felt I was in an earthly paradise.

The Poetic Key
Santiago, 1963-64

My first writing had the archaic flavor of Golden Age literature. I read like crazy, encyclopedias and comic books, novels and poetry, until I found two books that opened the door for me: the oral poetry of the Mbya Guarani, collected by León Cadogan,[4] and surrealist poetry by women, translated by Aldo Pellegrini.[5] Instinctively, I fused them. Hearing the way I read them I found "my" tone and "my" language.

---

4. Cadogan, born in Paraguay of Australian parents, was a self-taught ethnographer who collected and studied the folklore, language, and culture of the four groups that form part of the Guaraní Indian Nation of Paraguay. Vicuña is most likely referring to his collection of the oral myths of one of these groups, *AYVU RAPYTA: Textos Míticos de los Mbya-Guaraní del Guairá*. São Paulo: USP, 1959.

5. Vicuña is referring to Gisele Prassinos and Joyce Mansour, in *Antologia de la poesía surrealista de la lengua francesa*, Ed. Aldo Pellegrini. Buenos Aires: Compañía General Fabril Editora, 1961. She also refers to this anthology during the Barnard College performance in 1996.

Sonnets to Death
Liceo Manuel de Salas, 1965

In high school we had to memorize Gabriela Mistral's "Sonetos de la muerte," or "Sonnets to Death." That horrible poem, I thought. In Chile, to say something is "la muerte" is to say it is "cool." To learn a poem and recite it in class, however, was totally uncool. And yet, as I began to recite it, its power overtook me. The poem grabbed me and tore me apart. Now *that* was "la muerte."

Broken Song
Santiago, 1965

At my Aunt Lola's house I first heard that "*voz de tarro*," Violeta Parra's "tin voice." I had never heard such a dissonant, inharmonious, howl-like sound. It pierced me. In an instant, I recognized the true speech and sound of Chile. The ancestral memory suppressed by official culture was in that sound. From then on she became my compass.

Violeta was one of the first to record the *mestizo* songs of peasants. She played them on the radio, along with her own compositions. "Cultivated" Chileans made fun of her "*voz de tarro*." But when she killed herself, 60,000 people attended her funeral. Her work led to the New Chilean Song, a movement that influenced Latin American music throughout the continent.

The Diaguita Opera Singer
Santiago, 1965

My maternal grandmother, Teresa Arenas, was an opera singer, but gave it up to get married. After that she only sang at home. My mother learned from her and tried to teach me how to sing, but I couldn't carry a tune.

My grandmother, white as paper, dreamed herself European. But many years later, when I had my DNA charted, I realized that in reality she was a Diaguita from La Serena.[6] Our maternal lineage going all the way back to Lake Baikal in Siberia.

---

6. The Diaguita are a group of indigenous peoples whose culture developed in northwestern Argentina and northern Chile. La Serena is a city in northern Chile.

Brindis[7] Performance in Club de la Unión
Santiago, 1966

At Club de la Unión, we celebrated the 80th birthday of my grandfather, Carlos Vicuña Fuentes. Neruda wrote that my grandfather and his revolutionary companions had initiated the continent's most important movement.[8] Old friends from the 1922 rebellion were there—Santiago Labarca and other great orators. Each one of them toasted my grandfather, improvising an historic, political, or philosophical discourse on the decadence and imminent demise of the human race. When they finished, I stood up without invitation and began to speak. Women—much less teenagers—were not expected to speak during these toasts, but I had something to say. At that moment Santiago's plum trees were in bloom, and I had seen them on my way to the tribute. So I spoke of the common sap that ran through the trees and our bodies. From somewhere the power of resurrection and transformation was sure to emerge. I felt my words and saliva connected to the tree sap. Moved by my words, my grandfather grabbed the flowers from a table arrangement, crossed the banquet hall, and placed them at my feet, saying, "You are the next."

---

7. Brindis—a toast or dedication, which Vicuña considers a genre of oral literature in Latin America.
8. See Neruda's memoir, *Confieso que he vivido*. 1974. Barcelona: Random House. 2003. 319.

The Three Epiphanies
1966

That year three experiences gave my life direction:

EL DIARIO ESTÚPIDO

One day I was taking an afternoon nap and something grabbed me by the neck.

I got up and started to type: "*bagdad y los helicópteros. bagdad y los limones. bagdad y las personas que cantan. cuiden los ciruelos por si llegaren a dar frutillas.*" ("baghdad and the helicopters. baghdad and the lemons. baghdad and those who sing. care for the plum trees in case they bear strawberries.") They weren't words, they were realities that I transcribed onto the page. I knew that poetry had begun in me. That form of "hearing" went on until 1972, and came to an end as quickly as it had emerged. I called that work *el diario estúpido*, a 1,500-page text that contained poems, letters, and other forms. Only a handful of those poems were published, in *El Corno Emplumado* (The Plumed Horn) in Mexico.

LITTLE LITTER AND THE PRECARIOS

I was on a beach in Con-cón, when I felt the wind and the sea feeling me. I knew I had to respond to the Earth in a language that the tide would erase. I arranged the litter I saw strewn about. I called it *arte precario* knowing that art had begun in me.

WORD DIVINATIONS

I lived at the foot of El Plomo, the snow-capped mountain that overlooks Santiago, a sacred Inca site where a child had been sacrificed in ancient times.

It was late evening and I was in my bedroom, facing the mountain. Suddenly I felt a word entering my room. It opened up and danced, as a living being, showing me the forms it contained:

en a mor ados
en amor morado enajenados

in love forever
lovers ever foreign

I saw sixty words opening up. I called them "divinations" because each posed both a question and an answer.

I felt they came from the snow and stars, and that they enjoyed playing with me. The pleasure was mutual, but the laughter was mine.

Invention of the No Tribe
Santiago, 1967

My boyfriend Claudio Bertoni and I hung out with friends who were teenage artists and poets like us. One day I decided to call us *Tribu No*, the "No Tribe," since we weren't really a tribe, and we said NO to the world as it was. I wrote the "No Manifesto" and showed it to them. They laughed and paid no attention to it. But the name stuck, and the *Tribu No* became one of Santiago's legends.

"No activities" of *Tribu No*:

dance naked to Aretha Franklin
talk endlessly
read and write poetry[9]
paint
plant trees
knit sweaters
play games
watch TV
write theater pieces, manifestos, and children's plays

---

9. Around this time, poems by three members of Tribu No appeared in *El Corno Emplumado* (The Plumed Horn) #25, Mexico, January 1968. The only publication by Tribu No members was a mimeographed anthology titled *Deliciosas criaturas perfumadas* (Delicious Perfumed Creatures) (Santiago, no date/1970?), which was never distributed. It included Gonzalo Millán, Francisco Rivera, Marcelo Charlín, Claudio Bertoni, and Cecilia Vicuña.

The No Manifesto of Tribu No

Charlie Parker's no-movement, that is what we are in the warm and unsettled night of the South. As long as life persists in our individual, yet united, experiences, nothing will bother us.

We manifest no desire and no characteristic. We offer no manifesto to avoid being pigeonholed, and we are not afraid to pigeonhole ourselves—that would be as likely as suddenly becoming Polynesia's most daring parachutists.

We upset order with our exacerbated immobility. The no-movement is Charlie Parker's, John Coltrane's, Nicolás de Cusa's, Martínez de Pasqualiz's, Rimbaud's, Fhiloxenes's, and, most of all, André Breton's and Hölderlin's. In reality, we do not want to become demonstrators, since it would make the experience predominantly public.

We undermine reality from within, that is why we are subversive and loving. Furthermore, we are so minor and unknown that we delight in our freedom.

Tribu No's campaigns are not highly clandestine, and the only visible results for those of us who live-not the no-movement are our stupid works.

We hope to turn solitude into the world's new idol.

ha ha

We say no-thing. After speaking centuries of IT, IT remains a secret.
Our macabre intent is to leave humans naked, without preconceived notions, without conventional attachments-attire.
Have no fear. Our works will take years to manifest. We are not playing around.
The interior of the seed is soft.
IT is known only by living IT. Whatever IT is.
IT is yet to be discovered.

—Santiago de Chile, 1967

El Corno Emplumado and the First Translation
1969

In 1967 I discovered *El Corno Emplumado* in a bookstore in Santiago. I thought this was the most incredible journal, the only point of contact that existed between the U.S. and Latin American poetic vanguards. I wrote to them immediately and they published us. *El Corno* included letters by poets who corresponded with each other, creating an international community of friends. After the massacre at Tlatelolco in Mexico, Sergio Mondragón, a co-editor with Margaret Randall of *El Corno*, sought refuge in Bloomington, Indiana, and from there arranged for my poems to be translated into English. I traveled to the U.S, and the book was translated but never published. There were no readings organized. The true performance was traveling by Greyhound bus or hitchhiking across the U.S. and much of Mexico, visiting poets and artists affiliated with *El Corno.*

International Congress of Writers
Santiago, 1969

Writers from all over Latin America came to the meeting, among them Mario Vargas Llosa and Leopoldo Marechal.[10]

We were not invited, but showed up anyway, distributing handwritten leaflets that said:

Long live poetry. Down with functionaries who meet for cocktails with government ministers.

(A. Artaud) *Tribu No*

Long live poetry, the idiot Lao Tzu,
D.T Suzuki, Ernesto Cardenal.

(Nijinsky) *Tribu No*

Long live the displaced

Tribu No

Deserve your dreams

(Paz) *Tribu No*

Various writers later commented that this act was the meeting's only "literary" event.

10. Argentine writer of *Adán Buenosayres*, among other books, who died in 1970.

Bank of Ideas
Santiago, 1970

When Salvador Allende was elected President, some of my friends were among his collaborators, so through them I sent messages and suggestions: Just as there are banks for money, blood, and seeds, there should be a Bank of Ideas to gather and study the best ideas for the betterment of Chile.

The idea did not prosper.

Alfonso Alcalde and the First Sabor a Mí *Manuscript*
Santiago, 1970

Allende founded the press Quimantú to publish thousands of books that would cost "less than a pack of cigarettes." The poet Alfonso Alcalde directed it, and even though I didn't know him, I showed up at his office with my miniskirt and a 100-page manuscript of poems extracted from the "Diario Estúpido." Quimantú didn't publish poetry, but he and Carlos Droguett took it upon themselves to get the book published in Chile. With their help, I signed a contract with Ediciones Universitarias de Valparaíso. But the book never came out. Years later Alfonso told me that its eroticism shocked everyone who read it, particularly my uncle, who was a dean at the university. Effectively censored, most of those early poems remain unpublished.

The Seed
Valparaíso, 1970

I suggested to Salvador Allende that we initiate a collective work to green Chile, a movement to gather, study, and love seeds. Allende laughed and said "Chile is not ready."

Still, I gathered and sowed the seeds, and distributed them to shanty towns when they became saplings.

"Museo 70," First Poetry Reading of the Tribu No
Museo Nacional de Bellas Artes, Santiago, 1970

Nemesio Antúnez[11] had just become the director of the National Museum of Fine Arts. Newly arrived from New York he organized a sort of happening called "Museo 70," a one-night event that included Mapuche *trutrucas*,[12] Baroque music, modern dance, poetry, and rock music. He invited the *Tribu No* to read. This was my first reading ever, and five thousand people showed up. In front of that rowdy audience, I found my way of reading—it was coming from them. After each poem, the audience chanted, "More poetry! More poetry!" responding to our raw, foul-mouthed eroticism.

---

11. Chilean painter, 1918-1993.
12. A traditional horn instrument associated with the Mapuche Indians of Chile.

Julio Cortázar in Chile
Santiago, 1970

Writers and artists from all over the world came to Chile to participate in the "Chilean experiment." One day, expecting to take a math exam at the university, I found Julio Cortázar in the lecture hall, instead of my professor. He had come to talk to the students. I went to put a note in his pocket and Hans Hermann took our photo. (The next day, Cortázar slipped away from his official functions and spent the day talking to, and dancing with, *Tribu No.*)

Autumn, Museo Nacional de Bellas Artes
Santiago, 1971

I proposed to fill a gallery at the museum with autumn leaves, and Nemesio Antúnez agreed. I asked the gardeners of the big parks of Santiago to gather leaves for me. I also gathered a few. They brought them in big trucks and dropped them at the museum's door. My mother and I pushed them into the Sala Forestal (Woodland Hall) with our own bodies.

The day of the opening, Edmundo Pérez Zujovic, ex-Minister of the Interior, was assassinated. His murder was the first act of political violence that culminated in the 1973 military coup. The museum closed in national mourning.

The show opened two days later, without announcement. For that almost clandestine opening, my mother served *Torta de mil hojas*, or "Cake of a Thousand Leaves," while people waded through an ocean of leaves.

Dedicated to the "construction of socialism," the installation lasted only three days.

"Paintings, Poems, and Explanations"
Museo Nacional de Bellas Artes, Santiago, June 1971

A month later I exhibited my oil paintings, clumsy imitations of *mestizo* and Indian art of the 16th century, when native artists had to give up their art in favor of European techniques.

The paintings narrated my own history, interwoven with that of Chile, Salvador Allende, and the great rallies. Everybody asked, "What does this mean?" So I wrote absurd explanations and exhibited them along with the poems and paintings. The installation included broken furniture, lots of plants, and a folding screen titled "Little house to imagine what real situation suits me." The screen contained mirrors, and there was a little bench so people could sit and see themselves as part of the story. The overall effect was of a comic strip that included the visitors.

LONDON

The Scholarship
Santiago-London, 1972

After finishing school, I applied for a job in Chile, but didn't get it. Instead, I received a British Council scholarship to do postgraduate studies in painting at the Slade School of Fine Arts in London.

The day I left Chile, as I was saying goodbye to my parents at home, I saw, as in a vision, that the world I knew and loved would disappear. I cried all the way to Africa. When we reached Dakar, two rainbows enveloped the plane. Arriving in London, a wave of sadness met the airplane. I knew Europe was not the model it was made up to be. I went there because of Antonioni's film *Blow-Up*, but that was not the London I found. I clung tightly to the image of Chile and our "construction of socialism."

Shortly thereafter, I went to see Constantinos Costa-Gavras' film *State of Siege*.[13] Watching it I realized that death threatened our "revolutionary process." The film showed the CIA's intervention in Latin America and used Santiago as a prop to represent Montevideo, where a military coup had already taken place. My actor friends played the outlawed students. I suddenly knew it was not just a film, but a prophecy of what was to come. But nobody agreed: Chileans saw themselves as impervious to military rule. We had chosen to forget the military uprisings my grandfather and his friends fought against in the early 20th century.

---

13. The film premiered in London in early 1973. Set in Uruguay, but shot in Chile, *State of Siege* is a political thriller about the kidnapping of a U.S. official who is sent to Latin America to advise the secret police in methods of torture.

"pain things & explanations"
ICA, Institute of Contemporary Arts, May 1973

My studio was on Stepney Green, Jack the Ripper's street. My paintings and *precarios* were becoming witnesses to what was happening in Chile.

I called my first show in London "pain things & explanations," spelling out what was to come.

First London Lecture: "Art and Revolution in Chile"
ICA, Institute of Contemporary Arts, May 11, 1973

People wanted to know what Salvador Allende's Chile was like. The desire to say what I saw made me a speaker. In my first lecture, I said Chile was a place where art was the struggle to create a new reality, not a set of objects for museums and galleries.

The Chilean Military Coup
September 11, 1973

The day of the military coup, I was in my studio in London. Someone came to tell me Allende had died. I felt Chile had died with him. One hundred and fifty years of democracy over in one day. And with it, the dream of socialist democracy. I stayed up all night, painting Chile as a desert, with a colossal drop of blood falling into the sea. I named it *The Death of Salvador Allende.*

The military began to detain people. After torturing them, they would be dropped from a helicopter into the ocean. This is how they were made to "disappear." Among the disappeared was my uncle, Carlos Godoy Lagarrigue.

I Receive a Letter
London, 1974

The military raided my boyfriend's house in Santiago. They were looking for "subversive material." They found my paintings. And with a bayonet, ripped one of them, an image of a crossroads where everyone took off their clothes and made love.

Saboramí, Beau Geste Press[14]
Devon, England, Fall 1973

Felipe Ehrenberg invited me to publish an artist's book with Beau Geste Press. The press was located on a farm in Devon, where artists printed their own books. My book was about to be printed when the coup in Chile occurred. I changed its original contents, and the book became an urgent response to it. I incorporated materials found there: paper used to feed the pigs, leaves from the garden. Each copy of *Saborami* (250 in total) combined mimeograph and offset printing with other elements that varied from book to book: inserts of petals, letters and messages.

14. This book was reprinted by ChainLinks in 2011.

Class Struggle in the Pubs
London, 1973

The English unions requested Chilean speakers to talk about the coup, and the Chile Solidarity Committee sent me and others. The talks took place in the dark and foul-smelling back rooms or upper floors of pubs, where workers gathered to hear accounts of class struggle in Chile. It was in those spaces that my oral performance began to take shape, as I attempted to communicate the incommunicable.

On the opposite end of the spectrum, art schools invited me to talk about my work. I began to weave my autobiography, my art, and the history of Chile.

Artists for Democracy
London, July 1974

I met David Medalla, John Dugger and Guy Brett at a meeting of the Artists Union at the Institute for Contemporary Arts. Together we decided to start an organization in solidarity with Chile. I suggested we call it Artists For Democracy (AFD). We sent letters asking artists from all over the world to participate. We received responses and work from every continent, and organized the Arts Festival for Democracy in Chile at the Royal College of Art on October 14, 1974.

Roberto Matta came to London and created a mural for the event. Many other artists, such as Sol LeWitt and Julio Cortázar, sent work.

But the organization dissolved shortly after the festival.

Palabrarmas Performance
The Polytechnic of North London, February 1975

The military coup in Chile was a preemptive attack to "save" the country, based on a lie. One day in my studio, I suddenly *saw* the difference between truth and lies.

Both words opened up showing me their entrails.

They called themselves Palabrarmas or Word-Weapons: Words are the only acceptable weapons.

mentira: a lie

tears
men the mind
a part *tira*

verdad: truth

ver
gives sight
dad

I gave the first *Palabrarmas* performance projecting slides of artworks based on the words opening up. I dreamt of presenting the words as a visual language for the streets.

I imagined a new consciousness of language as the foundation for a liberated Latin American culture.

COLOMBIA

Arrival

1975

My study grant expired and I decided to return to South America. I traveled to Bogotá with five pounds sterling in my pocket. At that moment, Colombia was one of the few places in Latin America that didn't have a dictatorship. I got off the plane and was ecstatic at the sight of the mountains, the feel of the earth.

Censored Again
1978

I presented the erotic poems that had been censored in Chile to the Concurso Nacional Eduardo Cote Lamus de Medellín, a poetry contest sponsored by the Colombian government. Jaime Manrique Ardila, one of the jurors, revealed in a newspaper article that the poems had been denied the prize because of their eroticism. They became instantly popular. I assembled a trio with two musicians who played while I performed the forbidden poems. Censorship made me an oral poet. I'd kneel on the floor with my legs open, as if to touch the earth with a non-Christian prayer. The poems caused an uproar, and I started to make a living as a woman troubadour.

Cachaco Speech
Bogotá, 1979

People made fun of my Chilean pronunciation, so I learned *cachaco,* the way people in Bogotá speak. My Bogotá performances were a rapid clatter, violent, like the city's traffic. The fast rhythm of the pursued, escaping an ambush.

Palos de Guadua
1978

Traveling across the Colombian rainforest, I found a native bamboo, the *palo de guadua*. I incorporated it into my performance, carrying around this enormous cane on my shoulder. I hung gauze from it, constructing a ritual "home" or performance space. Many years later, I learned that pre-Columbian mummies had been wrapped in *palos de guadua*.

Santo pero no tanto / Saintly But Not So Much
Bogotá, 1978

I lived in the barrio Las Aguas, at the foot of the Guadalupe and Monserrat mountains, next to a factory that manufactured saints. My first documentary, *SANTO PERO NO TANTO,* was the story of my neighborhood—the way these saints rode around in buses.

Crimen Lechero / Milk Crime
Bogotá, 1979

The *Colectivo de Acciones de Arte* (C.A.D.A) in Chile invited me to participate in a project called *Para No Morir de Hambre en el Arte* (To Not Die of Hunger in the Arts) that would be realized simultaneously in Santiago, Toronto, and Bogotá. At the time Bogotá was enduring *el crimen lechero* (the milk crime), where merchants added paint to milk in order to increase profits, resulting in the death of 1,920 children. And the government was doing nothing about it. Around the city, I announced on posters the spilling of a glass of milk in front of the Quinta de Simón Bolívar. Twelve people attended. I spilled a glass of white paint on the sidewalk and wrote the poem on the pavement.

¿Qué es para usted la poesía? / What Is Poetry to You?
Bogotá, 1980

I decided to make a film asking the people of Bogotá, "What is poetry to you?" I formed a cooperative with a group of friends and went out into the street to film. It took me nearly twenty years to get enough funding to finish it.

NEW YORK

Arrival
April 16, 1980

A North American poet, Genie Nable, saw my performance in Bogotá, and invited me to come to the U.S. I performed in Tallahassee, then New York. Here, I met César Paternosto and stayed.

New York was the negative, or the reverse, of my world. If the Andean world was erasing itself, New York was all affirmation. To reverse the reverse was the work.

First Reading, Taller de Broadway, New York
May 1980

For that first reading I knelt on the floor and performed in my fast-paced, Bogotá style. A friend of César's said, "This chick's a metaphysical joker." Humberto Díaz Casanueva and Angel Flores[15] were in the audience, and they became my first friends in New York.

15. Díaz Casanueva was a Chilean poet and essayist who resigned as a United Nations Ambassador in 1973, and who also taught at Columbia and Rutgers Universities. Flores, born in Puerto Rico, was a translator, anthologist, publisher, and university professor active in the U.S. literary scene during much of the 20th century.

The Heresies Collective
1980

Lucy Lippard invited me to join the Heresies Collective, an extraordinary group of women artists. We met weekly for a whole year, debating issues and assembling the magazine, *Heresies: A Feminist Publication on Art & Politics*. For me, each collaborative gathering was an art form in itself, my best education and my entry into New York.

Alan Lomax & John Cohen
1982

In New York I encountered a music I had never heard before—the songs of the shepherds of the High Andes that NASA sent to outer space. In their voices was the ancient melodic matrix that traveled from Siberia to the Andes thousands of years ago.

La Wik' uña

1982

One day I found myself crouched at the entrance of the Holland Tunnel in New York. As I faced the truck lane, a song began to emerge. It was *La Wik' uña*'s song.

The ancient melodic matrix once more. I was a migrating animal, too.

Precario / Precarious
Arch Gallery, 1983

Faced with the extreme power New York and the U.S. exerted over the world, I remembered the fragile power of the *precarios.* I published my first book of *precarios*, and performed its silence broken by a few words, accompanied by the melancholic sounds of Pepe Santana's Peruvian reed flute, the *quena.*

Carnival Knowledge
1984

Lucy Lippard invited me to perform in *Carnival Knowledge*, an exhibition at Franklin Furnace.[16] I sat on the floor and projected slides of the ancient erotic pottery of the Moche in Peru, but my poems didn't correspond with them. So, instead of reading what I had written, I began to look for the missing lines. The absent poem, the search for what was not there, became my guide. Imagining the poetry and vision of the ancient Mochican poet-priestesses,[17] the work that history had erased, I improvised a verbal equivalent of the ceramics found in their tombs.

16. According to the invitation, Carnival Knowledge featured film, art, music, and performance that sought to redefine pornography through a feminist perspective. Vicuña's performance was titled "Eros del Sur."

17. Vicuña refers to the indigenous civilization that resided in the River Moche Valley on the northern coast of Perú, approximately between the first and eighth centuries AD, and that, in addition to architectural structures, left behind pottery depicting the human shapes of various archetypes, such as shamans and warriors.

Song Out
1986

I met Jerome Rothenberg at David Guss's home. Jerry asked me if I sang. I said only when no one was listening. He asked me to sing for him, and this high-pitched sound came out, a weird version of Violeta Parra's "Volver a los 17." A stuck record repeating just one line: "*como el musguito en la piedrá…*" ("like little moss on the rock"). While I sang, it felt as if the moss grew with the song.

Carmela Romero Antivil
Temuco, Chile, 1987

Sonia Montecinos took me to see the *machi* (shaman) Carmela Romero Antivil near Temuco. She performed shamanic healing rituals, songs, and ceremonies for me. She said I should begin to sing.

The Dark Room, Performance at Carmen Waugh Gallery
Santiago, 1987

I was to perform in Santiago, but I was afraid to sing. Urban poets don't sing in Chile. A centuries-old prohibition weighed on me. Plus, my 100-year-old grandmother, the Diaguita opera singer, was in the audience! So I turned off the lights and began to sing from a back room. Afterwards, my grandma said, "Mijita, don't turn off the lights, it's very scary."

First Non-Verbal Performance
Exit Art Gallery, 1989

Exit Art Gallery invited me to take part in a tribute to Theresa Hak Kyung Cha.

I placed a water fountain in the middle of the room, with a flame over it, and called it "Fire Over Water" in her honor. From the audience I threw tiny white rocks into the water. The rocks made a twinkling song. In her performances, Cha would give the audience white cards that read, "distant relative." Rocks, water, and fire are also our relatives.

The Decade Show, The Studio Museum in Harlem
1990

I still wanted to hide in order to sing, but this time there was nowhere to go. The Earth is transparent, says a Mapuche song. I began to perform while sitting on one side of the room, and sang as I walked to the stage with my kultrún. Once there, I took off my poncho of transparent gauze and threw it into the air.

Unravelling Words & the Weaving of Water
1992

Eliot Weinberger and Suzanne Jill Levine translated the poems, not from the written text, but from the stories I told of what was in the lines. When the book came out, Eliot and I went to California to perform. I put my water bowl on the floor and the hummingbird's song emerged, her trembling and fluttering sound, the light-worker's iridescence.

Allqa
Barnard College, 1997

Suddenly, I had no translator, so I began to improvise in a mixture of English, Quechua, and Spanish. The borders between the written and the oral began to shift. That day at Barnard College, there were two students with long hair in the audience, one with blonde hair, one with black. I invited them to join in. In Aymara, "*allqa*," the union of black and white, is the transformation of the world—the moment in which one begins to become the other.

cloud-net
1998

The true performance is that of our species on Earth: the way we cause suffering to others, the way we warm the atmosphere or cause other species to disappear.

I cover myself with clouds to feel like the Earth feels.

El quipu vivo / The Living Quipu
Celarg, Caracas, 2001

At some point, I began tying the audience with threads, or tying myself to the audience.

Who is performing: the poet, or the audience?

United by a thread, we form a living quipu: each person is a knot, and the performance is
what happens between the knots.

Empire
New York, 2002

Charlie Morrow invited me to perform with him on the observation deck of the Empire State Building. We arrived very early one morning, before the tourists. I began to weave and sing, while Charlie played his trumpet and bells.

The unsaid poem in my pocket said:
"Empire" means "to prepare against." The empire is fear.

Embracing our fear, a deep mourning emerged, the Skyscraper Blues.

Cecilia Vicuña in La Florida, Chile, 1950. (Photo by Norma Ramírez.)

Top: The Tribu No, Santiago, 1970. From left to right: Marcelo Charlín, Claudio Bertoni, Baby Mukti Ahimsa, Tao Rivera, Francisco Rivera, Sonia Jara, Cecilia Vicuña, Coca Roccatagliata. (Photographer unknown.)

Bottom: Cecilia Vicuña and Claudio Bertoni, Santiago, 1967. (Photo by Marcelo Charlin.)

NO MANIFIESTO DE LA TRIBU NO

el no-movimiento de charlie parker, ésto somos nosotros en la noche
desprendida y tibia del sur. mientras la vida magnífica perdure en
nuestras experiencias solitarias y sin embargo unidas, nada nos
preocupa.

no manifestamos ningún deseo o característica. no hacemos un manifies
to para no quedar encasillados. y no tenemos miedo a encasillarnos.
éso es tan difícil como que mañana mismo seamos el grupo paracaidis-
ta más osado de la polinesia.
perturbamos el orden con nuestra inmovilidad exacerbada.
además el no-movimiento es un movimiento de charlie parker, de john
coltrane. de nicolás de cusa y martínez de pasqualiz. de rimbaud y
philoxenes. más que nada andré breton y hölderlin.
en realidad no nos transformamos en manifestantes para que la experien
cia no sea preponderantemente exterior.
socavamos la sociedad interiormente. por ésto somos subersivos y amoro
sos
además somos tan pequeños y desconocidos que la libertad esnuestro
delirio, no sólo imag nativo. sino real.
las campañas de la tribu no son altamente secretas y los únicos
resultados visibles para los humanos que no viven el no-movimiento
son nuestras obras estúpidas. tontas e incoherentes, aunque no
necesariamente.

damos a conocer la existencia de la tribu no únicamente para que sea
notoria la gran inmovilidad y tambien dedicamos éste aparatito con
palabras a los que hablan demasiado y abusan de la compañía continua.

esper mos convertir a la Soledad en el nuevo ídolo mundial
jo jo
no decimos nada. dejamos todo igual, de modo que nadie pueda jactarse
de haberlo comprendido o agarrado. después de hablar siglos de Ello
permanece igualmente secreto.
el bonito anifiesto sirve para mostrar su intuilidad.
nuestro intento macabro es de ar desnudos a los humanos. sin ideas
preconcebidas ni atamientos convencionales. atamientos-vestiduras .
no se asusten, nuestras obras tardarán a os en aparecer: no estamos
jugando. la parte interior de las semillas es suave.
ELLO se conoce únicamente viviéndolo. sea lo que fuere ELLO
ELLO está todavía por descubrirse.

The No Manifiesto of the Tribu No by Cecilia Vicuña, Santiago, 1967.

1

MUSEO NACIONAL DE BELLAS ARTES
SANTIAGO - CHILE

SANTIAGO, 2 DE JUNIO de 1971

SEÑOR DIRECTOR DE JARDINES
PARQUE FORESTAL
PRESENTE

Muy señor mio:

La Señorita CECILIA VICUÑA realizará en la Sala Forestal del Museo Nacional de Bellas Artes una exposición.

Con este objeto necesita hojas del parque que le agradecería facilitar a la señorita Vicuña.

Le saluda atentamente,

MUSEO NACIONAL DE BELLAS ARTES
SANTIAGO DE CHILE

NEMSIO ANTUNEZ
CONSERVADOR

OJO

Cecilia me parece bien
visto y bueno
N. A.

Left: Letter from Nemesio Antúnez, Director of the National Museum of Fine Arts in Santiago, to the Director of Gardens of the Parque Forestal requesting that he provide autumn leaves for Vicuña's exhibition "Otoño." Santiago, 1971.

Above: Cecilia Vicuña, John Dugger, Kephas, Alejandra Altamirano, and unidentified friend during the installation of the exhibition "Arts Festival for Democracy in Chile," organized by Artists for Democracy at the Royal College of Art, London, October 14, 1974. (Photographer unkown.)

Page 106: Cover of the invitation to the Arts Festival for Democracy in Chile. Hortensia Bussi de Allende addressing the mass rally to protest the military coup in Chile, Trafalgar Square, London, September 15th, 1974. Banner by John Dugger of Artists for Democracy.

Page 107: First page of the letter by Cecilia Vicuña inviting artists around the world to participate in the Arts Festival for Democracy in Chile. Promotional stickers.

ARTS FESTIVAL FOR DEMOCRACY IN CHILE

organised by

ARTISTS FOR DEMOCRACY

at the Royal College of Art, London

14 October - 30 October 1974

open daily (except Sunday) 10 am to 9 pm

Señora Salvador Allende speaking before a mass rally in support of Chilean resistance, Trafalgar Square, London, 15 September 1974. Organised by the British Joint Labour Movement and the Chile Solidarity Campaign. In the foreground are trade union banners and in the background *Chile Vencera* banner by John Dugger of AFD

ARTISTS FOR DEMOCRACY

c/o STUDIO INTERNATIONAL, 14 West Central Street, London WC1A 1JH

30 July 1974

Dear friends and fellow artists,

During Popular Unity times Chile was a laboratory of invention. Art and Culture was flowering as never before. The people had the means to express themselves in all fields of creation; the press, radio, TV, the book, rallies, song, wall painting.

Artists were organised in brigades for painting. Were teaching, creating workshops, singing and dancing. Performing in shanty towns, industries and centres of Agrarian Reform. Creating mobile cultural units and tents of "Art for Everyone" which reached the remotest corners of our country. Museums were created and re-organised, open exhibitions and galleries sprouted everywhere, and all this joy, this freedom, was possible because we had conquered our political and economical independence.

With the Military Coup of September 11th 1973 all this came to an end. Our President Salvador Allende was assassinated and with him all the social, cultural and economic achievements of the Popular Unity Government.

Since then all freedom of expression has been suspended, culture is dangerous for the Junta, so they are trying to silence the people by practising exhaustive censorship and holding absolute control of the Media, the Education System and the Press. The new Chilean song has been prohibited, the wall paintings have been erased, there are no more art works and posters in the streets. Books, sculptures, paintings have been burnt, torn to pieces. Museums have been searched and sacked by the military.

Cecilia Vicuña reading a letter sent by artists imprisoned by the dictatorship on opening night of the Arts Festival for Democracy in Chile, Royal College of Art, London, October, 1974. (Photographer unkown.)

Cecilia Vicuña performing *Vaso de Leche* / Glass of Milk: a glass of white paint spilled on the pavement in front of the house of the liberator Simón Bolívar, September 29, 1979. (Photos by Oscar Monsalve.)

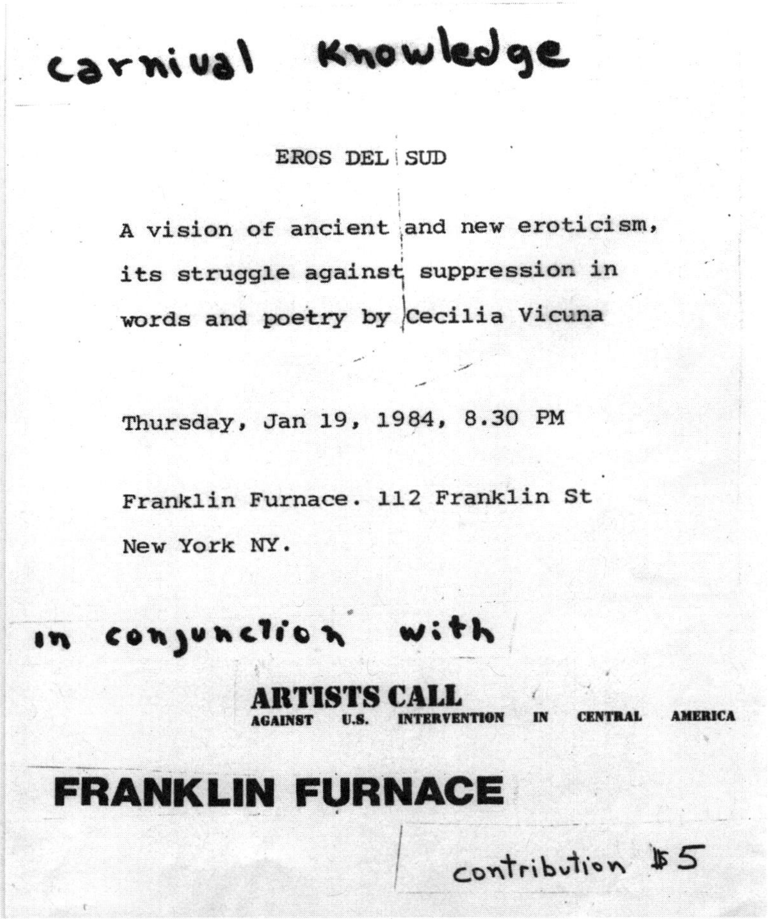
carnival knowledge

EROS DEL SUD

A vision of ancient and new eroticism,
its struggle against suppression in
words and poetry by Cecilia Vicuna

Thursday, Jan 19, 1984, 8.30 PM

Franklin Furnace. 112 Franklin St
New York NY.

in conjunction with

ARTISTS CALL
AGAINST U.S. INTERVENTION IN CENTRAL AMERICA

FRANKLIN FURNACE

contribution $5

Flyer for a performance at Franklin Furnace, at which Vicuña projected images of pre-Columbian erotic pottery from the Mochica culture in Peru while her poems re-constructed an imaginary poetics of the women artists of ancient Peru.

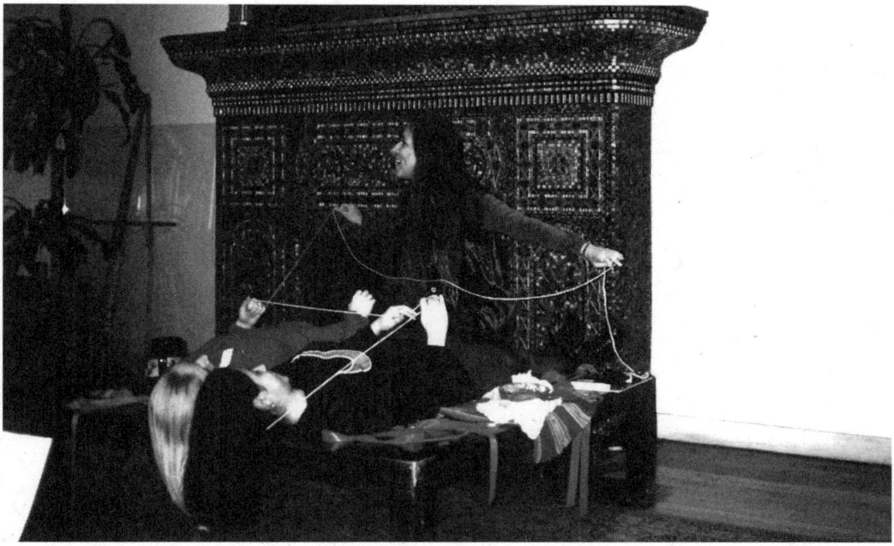

Cecilia Vicuña performs at Barnard College in New York City, 1996, improvising a loom with the bodies of two volunteer students from the audience. (Photo by Jorge Vicuña Lagarrigue.)

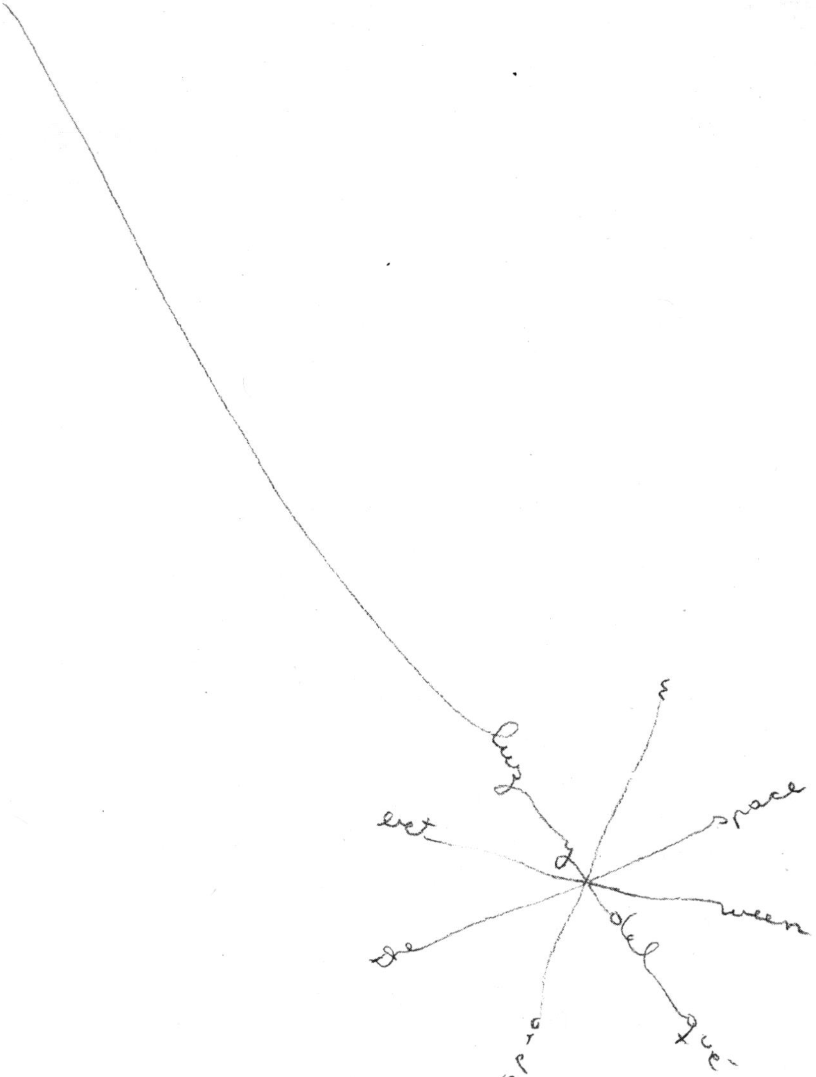
bet
space
ween
the
old

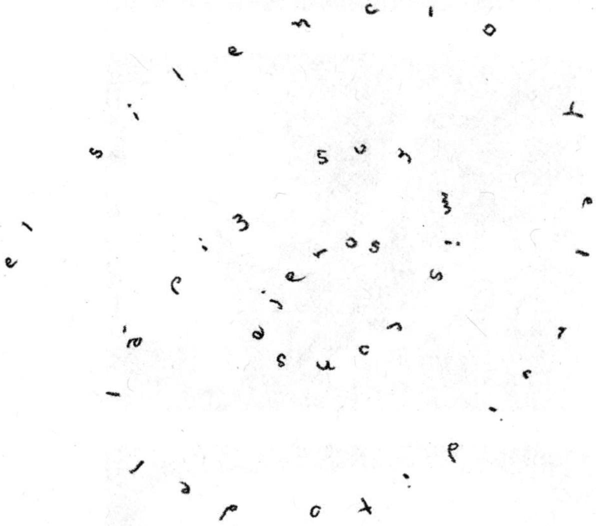

Two pages from *Instan* (Kelsey Street Press, 2002).

Still images from the video *cloud-net*, performed in New York City, 1998. In the background the Twin Towers of the World Trade Center; in the foreground the poem says: "we will all go away unless a new net worth is born." (Video by Francesco Cincotta.)

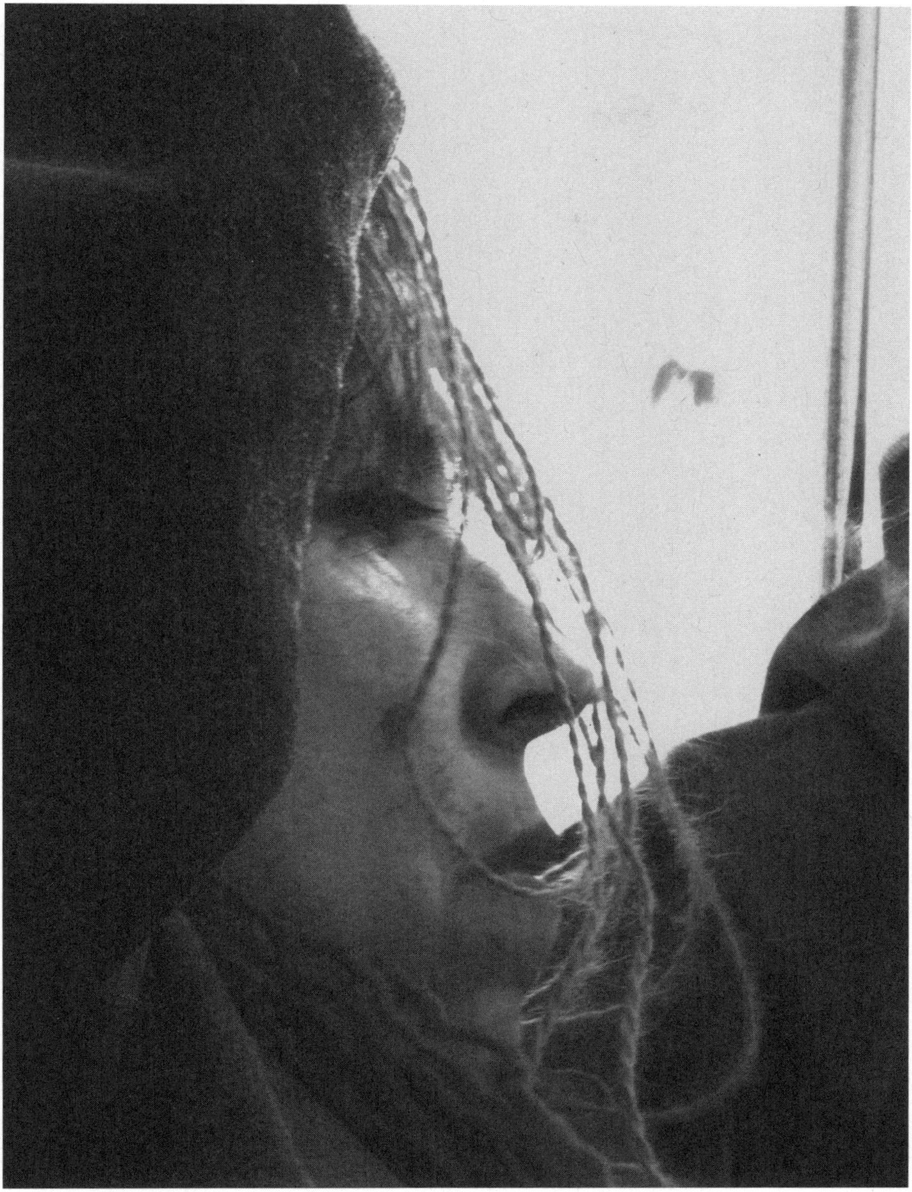

Cecilia Vicuña performing "Empire" at the top of the Empire State Building, New York City, 2002. (Photo by Francesco Cincotta.)

POETICS OF PERFORMANCE: TWO POEMS

El Quasar

La luz de un sonido, o el sonido de una luz?

Era su no ser nada aún, su "not yet" lo que me atraía.

Su ser "casi" un borde, un "a punto de suceder."

En esa calidad me mantenía, buscando una forma
antes de la forma.

La forma no nacía de una idea.

Era la idea desvaneciéndose.

Al nacer, el "no" la comprendía y aliviaba,
dejándola ser en su deshacer.

Un poema buscando su ser, el quasar no sabe buscar
sino el sueño del soñar.

The Quasar

Light of sound, or sound of light?

Its not-yet-being, its "no ser nada aún" is what attracted me.

Being "almost" a border, an "about to happen."

That quality kept me looking for a form
before the form.

Form was not born from an idea.

It was an idea vanishing.

At its birth, the "no" understood and soothed it,
allowing it to be in its undoing.

A poem looking for its being, the quasar can only search
for the sleep of dreams.

Un poema se convierte en poesía cuando su estructura
no está hecha de palabras sino de fuerzas.

La fuerza es la poesía.

Todos saben qué es la poesía, pero quién lo puede decir?

Su naturaleza es ser presentida, pero jamás aprehendida.

A poem only becomes poetry when its structure
is made not of words but forces.

The force is poetry.

Everyone knows what poetry is, but who can say it?

Its nature is to be felt, but never apprehended.

K'isa / Alangó / A Vibratory Disorder

A word moves
a bit of air
Nachman of Bratzlaw

God is the essence of the written letters
concealed in the dust of the poet's pencil
Sumana Santaka

To read a text in Thai is *tibot tack*: to smash it to pieces.

A *Tayil*, a song, is "the only material manifestation of the invisible reality," the Mapuche say.

"A song melts the boundaries between the worlds,"
Lawrence Sullivan says.

A vibratory disorder, an incantation bends time itself.

An image, too, is an "interference pattern," a rhythm born at the meeting point of light and eye.

"We don't see light, we see with the light," someone says.

A word in the air
lets you
hear the image
see the sound.

That's why in the Andes people say an image hears, a textile sees.
(You don't put on a mask to be seen, but to see with different eyes)

But there is no word for "beauty" (a song must never strike a right note)
you say *K'isa* instead,
the slow power to transform.
El suave endulzar de una fruta secándose al sol.
Hate and anger becoming peace and love.
A slow-drying fruit.

The spectrum is at work, too.

A degradation is an effort of light to unite shadow and light.
"The rainbow has a motor," they say.

To weave degradations is to weave an illusion that hits the eye as a *destello.*

"It is not to mystify with illusion, but to clarify the role of illusion in our perception of reality."

Alangó in Java, *beauty*, is not a noun, but a god, a divine manifestation.

Simultáneamente arrobado y arrobante, being in ecstasy creates the state.

K'isa, alangó.

THE QUASARS: SELECTED ORAL PERFORMANCES (1995-2002)

I called the performances quasars because they were quasi per, quasi form

They were nothingness itself in formation

—Cecilia Vicuña

THE POETRY PROJECT AT ST. MARK'S CHURCH
MAY 6, 1995[18]

A woman introducing Vicuña walks away from the podium. The camera's gaze is directed towards an empty podium and microphone. Silence. Then, chant-like sounds somewhere in the distance, out of frame. Frame opens and Vicuña approaches, singing, her hands folded behind her back, clutching a manila envelope. She sings.

...Basura sa liva
Basura sa liva
Ba su basura
Basura soy qori
qori wantu [19]

She takes papers out of the envelope and begins to read:

Una palabra
es tiempo

y sonido

tiempo
que respira

the word is time

---

18. Filmed by Mitch Corber.
19. Garbage spit / Garbage spit / Your garbage goes / Gold garbage I am / Gold berth." Vicuña begins with the word "basura," garbage, by hearing the English word "litter" in "litera de oro," which is the Spanish translation of the Quechua phrase "qori wantu," or "gold berth."

and sound
breathing

el sonido es un estado

y el estado es una estrella

a star is a state
and a state is a sound

A form of
con scious ness?
a mess?
together ness?
to gather ness?

Sound
in its ancient form
was swen

chan
tation
in cantation

sound
is enchanting
light?

There are two
South American myths
about sound
Sound,
the creator

One
accounts for the origins
of people who write
and people who sing

People in the rainforest
say
that when the gods
created peoples
they gave them
memory
so that
through sound
they could remember
all of their stories
but they created as well
some people
with no memory at all
these people they created
with a little notebook
in their hands
of course
you may guess
they were the Europeans — **audience laughs**
in the form of anthropologists
as they showed up
to the rainforest

Then there's another story
about sound
this one
is told
in Lima

When people
come down
the mountain
looking for work
into the huge city of Lima

the first thing they hear
is the roar
of the motors

It's funny but here in New York
we don't hear them do we? **looks around, as if trying to hear**

only faint in the distance
there they are
thank you[20]

Well, the sound
of all these machines
at work
in Lima
are the sounds produced from
by one being
that's the **Pishhh** ta ko
the **Pishhh** tako
that's eating
and feeding
on the blood
and grease
and body
of all the Indians

the Pishh ta ko

---

20. The sound Vicuña perceives coming from the outside is not audible on tape, but it must have been to members of the audience, who laugh when she says this.

Looks through some papers that appear to contain handwriting:

So here we are to hear
the sound
of the New York
Pishtako

In a whispery, sing-songy voice, almost like an incantation:

CAnta huevón
CAnta huevón
Dile al Pishtako
Dile al Pishtako[21]

Switches to a small notepad, and rips each one-inch sheet from the pad as she reads

Now I wish to tell you
a sort of not yet poem—
it's about Lola Kiepja
Lola Kiepja
was a Selk'nam[22] woman
and the Selk'nam
were the first
disappeared

---

21. Say to the Pishtako / Say to the Pishtako / Sing, you fool / Sing, you fool.

22. The Selk'nam people, also known as the Ona, once inhabited Tierra del Fuego (Karukinká, for the Selk'nam), an Argentine-Chilean island at the southernmost tip of Patagonia. Anne Chapman, who first visited Tierra del Fuego in 1964, writes that Lola Kiepja was "the only Selk'nam then still living who had been born before the colonization of her land, which began about 1880" (xi). She adds that Kiepja was also the last to live "as an Indian and the only remaining shaman." Kiepja died in 1966. See *Drama and Power in a Hunting Society.* Cambridge: Cambridge UP, 1982.

in Chile, that is to say,
they were a whole people
made to disappear

in order to grab hold
of their land, Karukinká
Karukinká,
which we now call
Tierra del Fuego.
These were not the Spaniards
in the 15th or 16th century
but it was us
contemporary Chileans
and Argentines
killing the Selk'nam
to grab hold
of their land
Karukinká.
The ranchers paid
one pound
per each Selk'nam man
who had been killed
but they paid two pounds
for each
woman
who had been killed.
And the proof of the killing
in their case
was their tits
cut
off.

Their tits.

They were proud of their tits—
to defend their hearts
against
the icy waters
when sea diving
around Karukinká.
Tits with designs
to talk back
to the stars
above
Karukinká.

Then
they were covered
by the missionaries
and no more right
to even speak.
Tits.
No more rights.
Tits.

In her last days

Lola Kiepja

who was the last
Selk'nam
the last person
Selk'nam
the last shaman
Selk'nam
in 1966
she started to record songs

for Anne Chapman[23]
and she loved la máquina[24]
la máquina
she said
mmmm
la mááquina
that was the tape recorder
she just loved it
and after recording one song
she would say
ORI SHEN
ORI SHEN
ORI SHEN:
that's beautiful
and then she would say
YI PEN
YI PEN
disgusting, disgusting

As an incantation:

Atina sentir
tus grandes tetas
mariscadoras
mariscadoras
mariscadoras

ya no
ya no
ya no
su mariscal

---

23. Selk'*nam (Ona) Chants of Tierra del Fuego, Argentina*. Recorded by Anne Chapman from March to June, 1966. Folkway Records: Ethnic Folkways Library, 1972.
24. The machine, referring to the tape recorder.

ya no
ya no
ya no

naúfragos flotadores
tus tetas
Lola

ya no
ya no
ya no

Switches to singing:

ya no hay mariscal

ya no
ya no
ya no
ya no

con ropa te encerraron
con ropa Lola
con ropa
con ropa te guardaron
te guardaron
te hicieron Lola[25]

Lola
Lola
mariscadora

25. According to Vicuña, *hacer lola*, literally "to make lola," is a Chilean expression which means "to crash" or "to destroy a person."

te hicieron
no
te hicieron
no
te hicieron
no no no
naúfraga[26]

aaah, Lola

Switching to larger notebook

Now I will read you a poem
an urban poem
of three women
this I wrote in the sixties
and
it was censored in Chile
but this is a recent translation
and this is in proper English so I read it to you
it's called "Mother and Daughter"
it's translated by Suzanne Jill Levine[27]

---

26. Try to feel / your large tits / sea diving / sea diving / sea diving // no more/ no more / no more / sea bounty // no more / no more / no more // your tits / shipwrecked / Lola // no more / no more / no more // no more sea bounty // no more / no more / no more / no more // they imprisoned you with clothes / with clothes, Lola with clothes / with clothes they kept you / they wrecked you Lola // Lola / Lola sea diver // they made you / no / they wrecked you / no / they made you / no no no / shipwrecked.

27. Levine's translation was first published in the *American Poetry Review*, May/June 1995, Vol. 24: No. 3.

The mother is as friendly as the daughters
she prostitutes herself
with ease
she's 20 years old
in each breast
and her nipples rise
agile
like race horses
her buttocks are sunken
and her maximum
aspiration
is to deny the existence
of all humidity
to take those worlds
off the earth
to let her daughters
be flat dolls

in the night
gusts of skin
take the house
all that was erased
begins to exist

crazed
the mother flings herself
upon her daughters
and rapes them

one after the other

since childhood they have known
no
other

treatment
today, reaching poverty
(puberty, I mean, or poverty)
with an apparent timidity
they look
as if they dominate
the world

Opens up her book, *Unravelling Words and the Weaving of Water:*

Now to pick up on the poems of David Trinidad
also about dolls
and about smoke
as if we had come to an agreement

well anyway I will read you another
girl poem
but this one
is a little more complicated
um
it's about a pun
in Spanish the word 'oro' means 'gold'
and also it's first person for 'I pray'
now the ancient weaver girls were isolated in a place called acllahuasi[28]
in ancient Perú
where they had no other mission
but spinning
and weaving
this golden thread
of Vicuña hair
now the whole poem is constructed constructed like two threads
the concept is that the two threads have to be

28. "House of Chosen Women" in Quechua.

one spun to the right
the other one to the left
so that they are in tension like lovemaking
to one another
this is what makes
the weaving
sacred

Reads:

Oro es tu hilar[29]:

TEMplo del siempre en he brar
arma tu casa en el mismo trez nar
teja mijita no más
truenos y rayos bordando al pasar
tuerce que tuerce el dorado enderezo el fresco ofrendar
ñustas calmadas de inquieto pensar
marcas señales
pallá y pacá
hilos y cuerda
los negros y los dorá
cavilan el punto
no se vaya escapar
hilo y vano
lleno y vacío
el mundo es hilván

Looks in book

pierdo el hilo y te hilacho briznar
código y cuenta

---

29. This poem and the translation that follows were published in Vicuña's *Unravelling Words & the Weaving of Water*. St. Paul, MN: Graywolf Press: 1992. 96-100. The translation is by Suzanne Jill Levine and Eliot Weinberger. In the transcription, I do not conform to the formal elements of the published version of poems, nor of their translations. Vicuña makes some changes to the Spanish version as she reads.

cómputo comunal
todo amarran
hilando en pos
cuerdas y arroyos
aunar lo tejido
¿no es algo inicial?

el cálido fuelle
oro templar
habla y abriga
el mejor juglar

Gold is your spinning

Gold
is your thread
of prayer temple
of forever threading eyelet
your house
built from the same braid
weave on
thunder and lightning embroidered
as you go
twisting and twisting
till the gold
rises
a fresh
offering
the unquiet thoughts
of the quiet weaving girl
marks and signs here and there
the threads and strings
black and gold

thinking
before
each stitch
not
to let it drop
a grid of empty space
a fabric of holes
the world
is a loose stitch
I've lost the thread
but I rag on
it's a code
an account
an account
of the people
tying it all
threading towards it all
streams and strings
the stars
the river weaves
the woven
woven into one.

Eso es todo
gracias

Returns applause and walks out of frame

BARNARD COLLEGE

NEW YORK CITY, NOVEMBER 16, 1996[30]

AaaaHHH
aaaahhhh

We're all tired aren't we

aaaaahhhhhhhhh

I'd like to respond to Rachel's
"nomadic
sheeee-mmmmer"[31] *hmmm*

"nomadic
shimmer"

but this one
between life
and death
and back

I like
to think
of our selves
as if we were dead

---

30. This performance-lecture, here in its entirety, was part of "America's Feminisms and the Poetics of the Avant-Garde," a panel organized by Rachel DuPlessis for Barnard College's 10th International Conference on Translation, November 15-16, 1996. The panelists, in order of presentation, were Kathleen Fraser, Susan Rubin Suleiman, Vicuña, and Rosmarie Waldrop. This transcription was made from an audio recording.

31. Vicuña is responding to DuPlessis's introduction, in which she explains, in relation to the title of the panel, that "*America's* means native-born and world-born, not a nationalism or a continent-ism, but a nomadic shimmer inside a specific civic and political location."

For now
we are people
but then
we will be only
voice
Navigating
we will go back
to the ancient
future
stream

stream of voice

When Rachel
invited me
to come

I thought
of all of us
of the lines
that began
in each one of the poets
present in this room
and each one
of all the ones that were reading
and the way
in which a phrase

—for example in a piece of paper
that Kathleen brought in
the dissolving string
from Barbara Guest—

each one of our lines

is continuing
and completing the next
so when we're all read
way back
in the future
HOW are we going to sound
speaking
to each other
becoming
once more
voice

And to respond and to echo
to this future
ancient
stream
of our voices
I wanted to go back
to the very very first time I came across it
But before I go into that
I wish to speak back to Susan[32]
to her mother
and the play with mother
Before we begin I'll remember my mother
I used to
write some text about her
where she would say:
YA MIJITA *vuelvo al tiro vuelvo al tiro*
Okay, baby, I'm coming back I'm coming back
Disappear for the rest of the day
THAT was her education
GREAT joy
GREAT fun

32. Referring to Susan Rubin Suleiman's talk prior to Vicuña's.

hmph
In the 60s
I'm a teenager and I'm living in Chile
and I discover this book
Antología de la poesía surrealista
translated by Aldo Pellegrini[33]
Dada and Surrealism in Spanish
my goodness
Dada
You have to figure out
I was fourteen and Santiago is a city
at the foot of these *huuuuge* mountains
Yet the city transfigures itself mentally
into a European city
Of course, everybody thinks this is so Western
DA-DA
DA-DA
nothing could be more appropriate
for us
And I remember the one poem
in this book
that did it for me
It was called "E pericoloso sporgersi"[34]
"E pericoloso sporgersi"
Kathleen would know what that means
this is a sign in Italian trains telling you not to put your arm like this
just outside the window you know
or your head much worse **audience laughter**
I remember this poem for like 30 years
and what it had done for me
And when I thought of this poem
I could see the arm, of course, outside the window

33. In Pellegrini's *Antologia de la poesía surrealista de la lengua francesa.*
34. "Danger: Do not lean out."

and the hair in the arm at full speed
and the skin becoming like a PRAI-rie of skin
and so
yesterday just before coming here
I thought to myself I better check it out

Of course it was nothing like I remember it **audience laughter**

Not a word of it

"E pericoloso sporgersi" was actually the second poem
and the one that I had forgotten
was the one that had the line

The line said
"no hay palabras
solamente pelos" **audience laughter**

hheehheee
no translation needed?
NOOO—let me translate a little
OK
SHE says, there are no words only hairs
hmmm?
So of course, I mixed them in
The poem I was reading in Spanish was written in English
by an Egyptian woman
born in London
Her name
is
Joyce Mansour

and I say this poem did it for me because in THAT poem

I found the door
to
write
exactly
the kinds of things that I perceived
and saw at that age
But the way it all began for me
was two years later
This is a lazy afternoon siesta
and all of a sudden
I get up
as if somebody or someone
or "what"
the "it" probably
from Charles's[35] poem
was holding me
from the nape of my neck
and *CRRRAKKK*
all of a sudden I begin to write
And the first words
that came in that poem
are in this little magazine from Mexico[36]

It says:
"*Baghdad* y los helicópteros
Baghdad y los limones
Baghdad y las personas que cantan"[37]
Baghdad, *hmmm*, Baghdad. Why Baghdad?

I thought of you
perhaps for you Baghdad

35. Referring to Charles Bernstein.
36. El *Corno Emplumado.*
37. "Baghdad and the helicopters / Baghdad and the lemons / Baghdad and the persons who sing."

would bring the image of Saddam Hussein
of what we now call Iraq

But for me, Baghdad in the 60s
what could it have been?
It must have been Scheherazade
the woman who saved her neck
every night
with her tongue

A forgotten scholar
a man called
Emilio García Gómez[38]
writing in the 40s in the South of Spain
said
that the melodic matrix
of the language we now call Spanish
began in Mesopotamia
began there
long before Baghdad was even called Baghdad
a melodic matrix
that traveled on the backs of camels
and horses all the way through Africa
into the Mediterranean
and into Spain
imagine that matrix
that melodic matrix
the sound innate
breathing in the songs
the mothers sing to their children
this matrix remains

38. In 1933, preeminent Spanish Arabist and translator García Gómez published *Poemas arábigo-andaluces*, an influential study of Arabic-Andalusian poetry.

the same as words
as syntax changed from one language to the next

The same and different
through all the migration of words
the migrations of sound

Then of course the meditation could go
into the
way all these Arab lyrics
so-called Arab
they were only Arab for a while
these lyrics
went into the Mediterranean
but would leave the Mediterranean behind
and now in the Andes
again
hearing my mother
and my mother is a dark woman
a Chilean woman
Chilean for generations
but she's Moorish
dark, hairy Moorish woman on one side
and Quechua, possibly
or who knows
Mapuche Indian
on
the other
side
so when she sung to me
two matrices
two melodies
were
mixing

the Andes
and Mesopotamia

Each one falling
and pushing the other
into place
for it is the emptiness
the void
the forgotten aspect
of each sound
that is probably
propelling us
into speech
as we search for memory
and oblivion
at once

words move in waves
of memory and forgetfulness

one giving birth to the other

A transmission
of voice: *"mi amor mijita*
mijita venga para 'ca"
the heart beat, all future rhymes
"mijito DESGRACIADO
VEN PARA 'CA
DESGRACIADO, hasta cuando me va a joder
este conche su madre"[39]
that's all you need
And the melodic matrix is in place

---

39. "My love, my girl / c'mere my daughter"..."Miserable child / c'mere / stop messing with me / you little brat"

As I speak to you in English I think
translation is possible because
thoughts are word less
and the voice is the transfiguration
of milk
the milk of thought
the milk of thought
you know going back into the sky
La via láctea, you know
is the mother pushing her tit up
you know
voice and words are feminine in Spanish
La voz y LA
palabra
but in Quechua they are neuter
because the voice as the person
includes both female and male
That's all.

HALLWALLS CONTEMPORARY ART CENTER

BUFFALO, NY, SEPTEMBER 27, 1998[40]

In the center of the screen, suspended in darkness, appears a bodiless white arm, perhaps a prosthetic or the plastic limb of a very large doll. This image goes in and out of focus as high-pitched singing or a kind of lament—***aaa eeeh A YA A YA A YA***—is heard somewhere in the distance, but getting ever closer. There is a shifting, a left-to-right adjustment of the videographer's gaze, an apparent search for the origin of these sounds, this song. The image first goes black, then white, refocusing on a single white thread seemingly tied to an imperceptible cloud in the distance. The camera follows the thread to find the silhouette of a petite woman doing slow, dance-like movements towards the stage. Her back to the lens, she is slowly wrapping the thread around her right hand, as if coiling herself toward the center of the room, or towards an off-screen universe. As she approaches the stage, she moves out of frame and can't be seen until she reaches what can now be clearly identified as the podium. And what once seemed like an amputated body part is in fact a microphone wrapped with a large, cascading piece of white, unspun wool. Behind the podium she tensions the white thread around both hands, creating a long blank between her fingers, and continues to sing.

She then greets the audience in a soft, whisper-like voice:

Buenas noches

By the time I get here it seems like a whole day has gone by,
no?

Buenas noches
buenos días

---

40. The transcription and description of the performance are derived from a video recording of the performance provided by Hallwalls.

Pauses momentarily, then moves a book to the side

Lezama Lima dice
"Weaving
is the birth
of light"

The light of the hand
spinning upright
a cloud of cosmic gas
begins to spin
matter
coheres
a galaxy
is born
the hand begins to spin
the word to think
pensare
in Latin
is to drop
the spindle
let it weight
pesar pensar
oro es tu hilar
hilo de orar
templo
del
siempre
enhebrar

hilo
hilito
treznar
la palabra

es silencio
y sonido

Picks up the book *Word and Thread / Palabra e hilo* and begins to read:

El hilo
lleno
y vacío
la tejedora ve su fibra
como la poeta
su palabra
el hilo siente la mano
como la palabra
la lengua
estructuras de sentido
en el doble sentido
de sentir
y significar
la palabra y el hilo
sienten

nuestro

pasar

The weaver sees
her fiber
as the poet
sees the word
her word
the thread feels the hands
as the word feels the tongue
structures of feeling

in the double sense of sensing
and signifying
the word and the thread
feel our passing
as I feel this
getting into my nose — **touching wool on microphone**
you know this
you can breathe it in — **fixing wool on microphone**

Estaba jodiendo no más,
estaba molestando la nube
todo el mundo me preguntaba
everybody wanted to know
about this cloud you know
what this cloud was
well, there she is
that's all she does
bother
and bother

In the Andes, people say
that unspun wool—
do you hear me, it feels like
this is in heaven — **pointing to the microphone**

someone fixes mic

People say that
unspun wool
contains the power
of the cosmos
because it's not yet—
it's nothing you see

it has not been spun
it's no thing
it's pure potential
pure future
pure being
pure nothing
a shaft of light
a line of light
running across
the worlds
creating the intermediate
space
a passage
between the worlds
but that's not the Popul Vuh
that's Socrates
speaking
of an ancient Greek
myth
he says is the core
the heart of the spindle
the heart
of the spindle
where the three girls are spinning
life and death
the shaft is light
and the whole spinning
is their voice
their voice
their song
their song
a tone is a thread
in Greek
tonos

Greek
tono
tono
is a thread
the tone of voice
speech is weaving
in Quechua
and tono
the thread of voice
a thread is not a thread
but a thousand
tiny
fibers
entwined
dissolving in air
a world begins again
El con
de la con-tin-ui-dad
is to hold with
el con, el con
no el que trampea
no el falso ni el mentiroso
el con del with
let's together
threads together
is to hold with
attention is a stretched thread
tendere[41]
mijito lindo
tendere
mijito no más[42]

---

41. Latin, "to tighten."
42. The con / of continuity / is to hold with / the con, the con / not the con artist / not the fake or liar / the con of the with...tendere / my dear son / tendere / at once, my son.

It's a strange thing
to work in this building
when you think
that the first puffs
of gas
of toxic gas
went out of buildings
just like
this Model T factory
you know
just spreading this gas
that's now
choking
the whole earth
So you come here
to create another sort of cloud
that's Sara's[43] work
another sort of cloud
come create
another sort of cloud

Sara and I were leaving
the building
the other day
going into the parking lot
it's warm and it's cool
at the same time
and Buffalo is full of clouds
this is a cloud city
and we go out of the building
and Sara says
you know
when you touch something

43. Sara Kellner, who at the time was Visual Arts Director of Hallwalls.

you don't
really
touch
it
because we're made
of the same
molecules
you
are what you touch
it is just the meeting
of two forces
she said
another man said

I'm not really here
I'm only the shape
of the emptiness
that holds me
the inner space
of those dancing
molecules
again
only in music
the tone, think of the word
"el mole"
"el mole"
no la chanchería para comer
el mole culo
el mole culo
él mueve el culo[44]
so you live to die

44. Here Vicuña is playing with the word molecule, which looks like it contains three Spanish words: mole, a Mexican sauce; moler, to grind; and culo, ass. She transforms mole to mueve, and the word molecule becomes, "he shakes his ass."

and to let music
go on
let
another form
of emptiness
come
which brings to mind
think of the primitive barbarians
that went out in the 15th century
all over the world
to conquer the world
as primitive barbarians
thinking
that everybody else
was a primitive barbarian,
involved in what they called
ancestor worship
c'mon
ancestor worship—maybe people
were a little more aware
and feeling
the place in time
the place
in the line
in the shaft

we will come
we will come

The people in Africa
say
we
are preparing

to become
an ancestor
every day as we make breakfast
we are preparing
to become
an ancestor
and the Incas thought
of the ancestors
as seeds
seeds of the future
there was not a word yet
for gene
gene
el genio[45]
el gen-io
el genio
el genio del mundo
what are we doing
perhaps
to be a line
is to create
a future meaning
why
why
a way in which
you were remembered?
Acts are descriptions
a writing in real time
acts

takes out some loose sheets of paper and begins to chant:

---

45. *Genio* is Spanish for genius; it can also refer to someone's temperament.

Illapa I-llapa Illapa Illapa
I I I lla alla pa IIIapa Illapa
I I I I I lla pa
I I I I lla pa iii la pantac
Illapantacc Illapantacc Illapantacc

They say that a woman should never
ever, ever, ever, ever, ever
pronounce that word
it's a word that brings bad luck
to women
because this is not a verb
it it's a word that compounds
many many many
verbs
one of them is
the trueno
the relámpago
el rayo[46]
Illapantac
Illapantac
don't let me say it
Illapantac
Illapantac
Illapantac

As the stormmm
came in this morning
you could feel the Illapantac
the Illapantac
in Inca poetry
they say
los versos
son pocos

46. *Trueno, relámpago*, and *rayo* translate to thunder, lightning, and thunderbolt.

pero muy compendiosos
pero muy compendiosos
the verses are very very very small
very short
but they contain
they contain
as many verbs
as many powers
as many rays
as many thunders
as
possibly
can be
included
in
them

fading into a whisper

And also

I I have the feeling that

looking down at hands and creating with the thread a sort of cat's cradle

Dennis and Barbara Tedlock
would be here
so
I didn't want to make
an homage to them
but you know these things happen
And
em,
as I was thinking of the storm this morning
I remember once
that we were together

in Colorado
in Boulder
and—we decided to go see the snow
up in the mountains
and they said to me
this is not something very wise
because you will go get
the snow
the glacier
and if we touch it, we will bring the storm
Soon enough when the moment came for them to give their poetry reading
down in the city where we were
as soon as they got into the tent or even before—
rays and thunder started storming down

gesturing with hands the storm coming down

And so, instead of saying anything
I will say I-I'm doing a little book now[47]
and the book begins with a line
Dennis
I hope I'm quoting by memory rightly—
he says

um, let's see
my memory
it says
um
midday
umm
you correct me Dennis
it says
midday is everywhere
but day

---

47. Vicuña is referring to her book *El Templo*, which includes art by Manel Lledós. NY: Situations Press, 2001.

is nowhere to be seen
No? looking up, smiling towards someone in the audience
Is that right?
Ok.

And because male without female
is no thing,
then
Barbara comes
and in her book[48]
she mentions
one word
which I may pronounce badly in Maya
which is K'ij
K'ij is day
but from this word
two words are derived
K'ijilabal
maybe I say it wrong
And K'ijiloxic
maybe I say it wrong
which is to day love
hmm
which means prayer

And to day count
which is another form of thought
to divine
so the poem begins—
El templo es el día
y orar es diamar
estar en elll

48. She is referring to Barbara Tedlock's *Time and the Highland Maya.* Albuquerque: U of NM Press, 1982.

sabiéndolo

The day is temple
and to pray
is to day
being
knowing

And for some reason when you come here
and you are struck by the lights
And you are struck
by the presence of everybody
you start sweating
like a dog

You can see it
don't you
and so
you say
la tierra
es el agua
corriendo en la piel
lágrima el agua
tierra el llorar
la tierra del poema
es llorar
la tierra es el agua del llorar

moves sheets of paper aside

Luis Gómez.

This is totally at odds
but I live in Manhattan

part of the year
and
I have always been fascinated
by the holes in Manhattan
you know, you walk by and there are these
tremendous holes
sometimes water comes jumping
out of it
hand goes up with thread cascading down from it
as a geyser, you know, and it's because the water pipes have exploded—
they are from the 19th century
and of course sometimes water is rushing down:
sometimes people are falling in
sometimes people are coming out

In any case, there was this man
called Luis Gómez
and this happened only a few blocks
eh, no, not even more than a few blocks
a block and a half exactly away from my home
And Luis Gómez
he was an illegal worker
And he was working in one of these holes
And then apparently
he went into having
a nice nap
And another worker came
and without noticing
that Luis Gómez was there
came and threw all the rubble
on top of Luis Gómez
and killed him
And nobody notices
and the hole was covered

and everything was okay according to the
workers
except that Luis Gómez
had a brother
and the brother came later and asked
where is Luis Gómez
nobody had seen Luis Gómez
And somebody had the hunch
I believe it was his brother
that he might be in there
so they started to dig a hole
and there he was
he was crushed like a little mummy
puts hands wrapped in thread against her head, gesturing sleep
a little body
inside the hole

So this is for Luis Gómez

pauses, looks down, and sings as in a lament:

Luis Gómez Luis Gómez Luis Gómez Luis Gómez Luis Gómez
Luis Go me eh eeeeeeeeeee eeehhhhhhhhhhhhhhhhhhhhh eh eh eh eh eh ehe...
Luis Gómez Luis Gómez Luis Gómez...

te taparon como un hoyo
Luis Gómez te
taparon
como un hoyo Luis Góm—ez
tu eras el hoyo

tra gando tierra
tu eras el hoyo
Luis Gómez Luiiiisss Go—méz
Luis Gómez
Tu pe-queño cuerpo
mal-her-iiiii-d-ooooo

aahhhh
perdona perdona

shifting papers on the podium

I'm sorry
if this is all like messed up like that
I've been working for a whole week you know
creating all these holes over here
and so
I wanted to respond to some of these strange questions
that people have asked me about the net
and I
have been
thinking
And a piece will probably come of this
a longer piece
But thinking of the people here in Buffalo
I-I I was noting
there is a wonderful book by a woman
an Argentine American
these people of confused identities
like so many of us
who comes and goes

and she went to the north of Argentina
and discovered
that most of the anthropological
em, writings about the Andes
were a little off and this
not only a little off
shall we say—
simply because
there was not a connection
with the body
as the body is perceived in the Andes
and she came up with these wonderful perceptions of the body
and so
she has a reading
her name is Barbara Classen[49]
and she has a reading of the body in the Andes
and she says something so exquisite
and
probably
true
she says
la escritura
en el mundo Inca
es percibida
como un desorden sensorial
writing is the sensorial disorder
if that makes any sense in English
not
like
the quipu[50]

---

49. Vicuña means Constance Classen, who wrote *Inca Cosmology and the Human Body*. Salt Lake City: U of UT Press, 1993.

50. A quipu is a "device consisting of cords or threads of different colours arranged and knotted in various ways, used originally by the Incas of Peru and the surrounding areas for recording events, keeping accounts, sending messages," etc. (Oxford English Dictionary). See also Maria Damon's

which is a three
dimensional record
of the instant

Also coming here

there were three more weavings
I should talk about
before going away.
One is a story.
I don't know if this is a poem
or it's just an Illapantac
and what it is
I was in Buenos Aires
and in Buenos Aires I was asked
to do a reading
at the new museo there
so I took a bus
and I had had a dream
and in my dream
I just remember
as we were sitting
a thread waving like that **pulls thread which is tethered to something**
was in my dreams **outside of the frame**
so I saw
the buildings
and with threads waving outside
and in the dream
this was a work
that somebody else had done
and of course I thought my god
this is so beautiful
so fantastic

---

response at the end of this book.

the threads
coming out of buildings
like that
So I take
I'm awake now
and I'm taking the bus
and I'm riding the bus
and all of a sudden
and what do I see?
Threads coming from building
to building
but they were
not empty like this, the
threads have pictures
and photographs on them
and what is it?
it's the photographs
of the desaparecidos
of the people that had been killed
by the military
so the women
had devised
a thread installation
to run
all across
La Avenida de Mayo
between the Congress
and the House of Congress
threads
white threads
with the pictures

there
hanging

so I arrive in the place where I had to do
my poetry reading
and I all I can do
is think is think of the story
that was in El Diario Clarín
that morning
and the story
is like this:
a poor woman
wanted to go
visit
her son
on the other side of the mountain
poor people only wear
alpargatas
these are not even shoes—
it is sort of espadrilles
And the sun is very strong
in the Southern Hemisphere
because of the ozone hole
so this woman started her journey
and she was blinded

A moment came when she couldn't see her way
and she got lost
in the mountain
and she spent three days
and three nights
totally lost
Her son on the other side
of the mountain
started to realize
that something was wrong
and started to look

for her
and all he could find
was
the loose
threads
of her espadrilles
that she had been destroying
as she walked looking for him
until he finally saw a pattern
of all the loose threads
and started to follow
the
broken
threads
until he finally
found her
and there she was
alive
and the way she had survived
is like this:
when she was blind
it had rained
another
storm
came
and through touching the ground
she felt
that where animals
had stepped and made little holes
like this
of their footsteps
water had gathered
so she went down
like this **drinks from a cupped hand, a string dangling from it**

and drank the water
from these steps

Mother and son returned

Putting some papers to the side, and looking at sheets of paper

There's another silly poem I wanted
to read you
but I don't know
um, these poems have a bad habit, ah

Puts on glasses for the first time in the performance

I can't even see them
The question is that they continue to move
and this probably happens to most poets
that their poems
are too wavy,
and especially if they're in a language
that you don't really grasp completely
like English, ah

but this had to do
with, um,
Chris Borkowski
who is somewhere here
who works
in the video
and I

were creating a sort of video poem[51]
which was shown last night
and this poem is is is a sort of
adivinanza[52]
and the way it is

you know because of the World Wide Web
you have these three w's
WWW, which is like a wave in itself
but a wave that nobody sees
and nobody associates
with any wave of course
and while we were doing that
I remembered
if you see the film
you will see that in this film
three girls,
not the same girls as in Socrates's story
but it turns out that it may be
may be
may be maybe
Well in any case these three girls
were weaving by the Hudson River
and as they weave
and wave
the other girls are blading throughout
so it says:

the weavers waving their blades
the river weaving its waves
the three young girls exciting her feet

---

51. The video Vicuña refers to is *cloud-net.*
52. Riddle

as the river zig zags
its waves
criss crossing
its waves
the waves in the river
many
many
layers of waves
some   under   currents
belonging to the movement of waves
in relation   to the earth
the earth moving its waves
blading across   the girl
weaving waving

And now just to say good-bye

I admire my colleagues   while flipping through pages of a book
who put here the little watch   motioning to a corner of the podium

I could not do that
because then it would be looking at me
and then I would get too confused—   laughing
I would not know what to do
So um then eh
we will make just a little song
from
this old book
which I have probably
read

to
you
before
and it is also about the cloud net
in a way

eh—
people ask
what is this cloud net?
and well, eh, the cloud net
the cloud net
and ah
one thought is that
um, the Earth has lost
its cool,
we say
the weather is getting too hot
and too cold
just like people in the rainforest say
you know
the law of moderation
is rain
rain and clouds
are the law of moderation
first the trees go
and then
coolness is gone
coolness is gone

still flipping through a book, but not reading from it

so because of that they say
mist
is the semen
of the mountains
where the streams are born
mist is the semen of the forest

where coolness
is born

Phuyumama licenciakimanta[53]
madre de las nubes licencia pido para pasar

shifting into a higher pitched voice, while reading rapidly and rhythmically:

Neb lini lla fibr OsA
Neblinilla fibrosa
neblinilla ciempiés
fragando frugando
su fertilidad
Cuiden sus llamas
Cuiden su lisor
Que hermoso
qué hermoso
Dijo y despertó
Así lo traía
de vuelta en visor
Así lo subía
brillando en su haz
Fueguito sagrado
Ofrendilla de mies![54]...

53. From "Phuyumama licenciakimanta" to "Ofrendilla de mies!" is a version of a poem that appears in Vicuña's book *Unravelling Words & the Weaving of Water* (109-110). A translation by Suzanne Jill Levine appears in the book.
54. I transcribe only part of this chant.

ART IN GENERAL

NEW YORK, NY, MAY 19, 1999[55]

With one end of a thread in her hand and the other tied to her ankle, Vicuña hands a segment of it to a group of people in one corner of the room. She then pulls the thread towards the center of the room, creating a v-shaped tether between audience and performer. Beneath her installation—a net of threads that sags from the gallery's ceiling—she arranges a small pillow, where she'll sit for the performance. What follows is a compendium of creaks and inaudibilities.

a   we core se
______________messengers of   ______________——-able
deathless force_____________the mysterious steps
____fog
________________________________shall change
the suffering earth the light
shall not______________________________
               in the cloud-net of her hair
a music of griefless things
griefless things shall weave shall weave shall weave

—————(singing) ***un poquito un po . quito un poquito***

kkkkrrrkkkkrrrkkkrrrkkkkrr)   you don't hear me?
you hear the floor?

(audience: "yes")

la puerta interior de la palabra_______________

---

55. This transcription of the first few minutes of Vicuña's performance (filmed by Francesco Cincotta), which formed part of her cloud-net installation at Art in General, reflects gaps of audibility or intelligibility caused by squeaky floors, people getting off a nearby elevator, and poor acoustics.

esta
art art

the arms spinning
setting the warp
____________an echo of the hand

are in wri———
echoing

or is a wa——
echoing the arm

——ar——-
the word or______
only a music of hands

manos__________
crkkkkkcccrrrrrkkkkk
crkkkkccrrrkkkk iiiiikkkkiiiiikikik ik ik cc rrr kkkk

When I first came to this space, I thought I wanted to do a piece that would be just the squeaky floors and if I ______________you see this is really happening __________noise this__________________
I don't have to do anything
it just happened.

KRANNERT ART CENTER

UNIVERSITY OF ILLINOIS AT URBANA-CHAMPAIGN, SEPTEMBER 21, 1999[56]

Silence on audiotape for several minutes, then the sound of a gourd being shaken in the distance. As she approaches the microphone, chanting can be heard, getting louder with each step:

YUUUUU-HAAA
YU U U U U U U U-uuuuuuuuu....

UTU UTU UTU UTU UTU...

YA está bueno váyanse

Hello how are you?

applause

Now I'm finally hot
you know that over there it was warmer than over here
it felt so cold when I came in
so
I'll undress but only a little of course

just to begin
And I'm so happy to be here
most people always say that
I don't know if they really mean it

56. "Seed Speakings: The Potential of Some Ancient Ideas Concerning Seeds," performance-lecture and slide show at the Krannert Art Center (George A. Miller Committee Series).

but I do

I hope you will see
why

I'm coming
from a thirst
a hunger
that has no name
we call it
AAArt
we call it
poetry
or we call it
beauty
for lack
of a name
the three words
only mean doinngg,
making
a thirst
for a nectar
a juiccce
an ambrosia
that flows
from the doing

like a streaaam into the ocean
of all
other
doings
The oldest form

of the word 'sed'
thirst
of the word love,
'luva,'
was thirst

a thirst

The first prayer ever recorded
said
'let me see
your beauty'

A prayer recorded in an Egyptian
tomb
the oldest
written
prayer
we know
the oldest reconstructed root
for beauty
being *dw-eye*
in Latin, *beare*
to make
blessed
a blessed making,
in Greek
du-na dunasthai
to be able
to be able
to bless
as you make
let the making
be the blessing

not apart,
away from life
say all the other cultures
that never
invented
a word for beauty
a word for art
that's what they meant
for the
ecstatic
making
that we call
art
So I undo the word art
and play with it
what matters
is that we never agree
THAT is what it is
THAT is what keeps us
going
continue to come back
the UNdefined
UNdefinable
the UN
the UN the
the UN
in the play
when you say art
you're really saying *ar*
as in the *arm*
the art
coming down the arm
setting the warp in a loom
"odor" and "right" from the same

root
the odor of the world
the true art
that is what perhaps was meant

What do we do
with our lives?
el arte es tratarte[57]
we say
el arte es tratarte
we say

But now

I'm not only coming
from that thirst
I'm also coming from New York
as you all know
I'm coming from the heat
the asphyxiating heat
of the summer
this was the hottest summer
we have ever
had
we come from the heat
the asphyxiating heat
I say this was the first summer
of the future
people couldn't cook
where I was in Long Island

57. Art engages you, or art talks with you.

because water
was already contaminated
and people went about
this business
as if nothing was going on
with water coming out
of the tap water
totally smelly
totally dead
already
then you couldn't go about
at dusk
to see the sunset
for fear of the mosquito
perfectly normal
perfectly normal
New York
the first summer of the future
you would go out
on a stroll by the river
at the Manhattan South End
where I live
and at high tide the waves
would come lapping
on top of the cement
lapping up
saying I'm coming up
I'm coming up
of course the President said
we are going to release
the secret papers
saying that Antarctica is about to fall into the sea
no one needs any secret papers
everybody knows this

everybody knows that Antarctica
a good part of it is about to
kkkwaaak

onto the sea

the water
lapping
us

Bill McKibben[58] I'm sure you know him
he was telling a story
of how in a place in Tibet
people started planting trees
and this had changed
the speed of the wind
so people instead of being attacked
by a brutal wind
would be
TOUCHED
by a soft wind
stopped by the trees

In Lake Titicaca people are doing what is called
Waru
Waru
Waru Waru means to reconstruct
the ancient raised fields
once they started doing that
the temperature around Lake Titicaca[59]

58. McKibben, the author of several books about the environment, including *The End of Nature*. (NY: Anchor Books, 1997), which regards global warming, writes in the *New York Review of Books*, "Reforestation in many areas [of Tibet] has been so successful that wind speeds in the Lhasa valley have decreased by one mile per hour" (46 (1): Aug 12, 1999).
59. Clark L. Erickson, who researched "waru waru," the prehistoric "raised field" agricultural

started to become very soft
not so much hot
not so much heat
started to become
soft as a caress
so I said
this is our true medium the speed of the wind
this is our true medium
the heat
the warmth
the softness
of the weather
or the VIOLENCE of the weather
Nazca—I want to show you
a first image

singing:

la noche se está lle gan do
la noche se-stá llegan doooo

la no-cheeeee
la no-cheeeee
la noche se está llegaaaaan do

la noche se está llegaannndo

---

system ("elevated planting platforms [that allow for] drainage, improved soil condition, and improved temperatures for crops") in the Lake Titicaca Basin in Peru and Bolivia, concluded that this ancient technology was superior to modern methods. In 1982, he and his colleagues formed the Raised Field Agricultural Project, which combined the efforts of scientists with local indigenous farmers. See "Raised Field Agriculture in the Lake Titicaca Basin: Putting Ancient Agriculture Back to Work." *Expedition 30.1* (1988): 8-16.

It is difficult to speak
and to sing
and to show images
the three things
collide
and
you are never settled in any one of the three
but people
when I came here
asked
uh, whether I was going to show some of my work and I said not really
but I had brought one image
so instead of speaking
of the work we're going
to do here
in the future
I will speak of this last piece
this piece is called
cloud-net
el aguanta nubes
el tejiendo nubes

and it is the last piece
I did
as Leslie was saying
this piece is just
a piece of cloud woven
and what it is is the
un-s p u n wool of sheep
as you know unspun wool is not fit
for weaving
and we consider this to be
a cloud

like a cloud of cosmic gas
before anything exists

Weaving clouds
against death

and precisely because
of this heat
I started to weave
clouds

to bring back coolness
into the earth
weaving clouds against death

ok, you can turn it off
I don't know how to turn this off though

thanks

hmmm
now we are attacked by the light

ahh I know
we will want the lights off again
you see
I didn't bring the little miner's flashlight

okay turn it off again please
okay

okay you can turn it off
shall we get lights
to attack us again
okay good

you can turn it off for a while

good

That
little
round
piece[60]

for me that piece
is bound in the earth
with a future
image
of the earth
a female version
of its emptiness
as Pachamama[61]

---

60. The Nazca ceramic piece Vicuña refers to is described by Alan R. Sawyer as, "A double spout bottle having a plain undecorated spherical body with a hole through its center." It was created by the Nazca people, South Coast of Peru, during the Early Nazca period, from 200 BC to 300 AD. See Sawyer, Alan R., *Ancient Andean Arts in the Collection of the Krannert Art Museum.* Urbana-Champaign: U of IL Press, 1975: 98.

61. Vicuña defines Pachamama as "the Mother of spacetime, the creative force that makes the Earth possible (in other words, an abstract concept)." The term is commonly used as "Mother Earth."

a wounded version
of its Ozone hole
a wholing
version
a healed
version
of its coming
out
of the (w)hole
when we see it
hole
just the 'w'
a world of weaving
the we we we
turns it around
the we we we
in weaving
as in World Wide Web

our death
the death of the Earth
turning
it
around

The piece, though
is a piece
that thinks of itself
in a manner
entirely different
this is a piece done by the Nazca people
probably at the end
of the last centuries

before
what we call
the
Christian
era
People here at the museum—
Alan Sawyer for example in a note says
"The stone head of an implement used to break up
clods of earth"[62]
once the earth
has been loosened
clods of earth
some people think
that clods
are the first root
for the word cloud
clods of earth

some other people say
that the Nazca people
are the least
militaristic
in Ancient Perú
so that this piece
does not
really
look
like a weapon at all
but a piece
for planting the earth
planting the earth
but when you touch it

---

62. Sawyer, Alan R. *Ancient Andean Arts in the Collection of the Krannert Art Museum.* Urbana-Champaign: U of IL Press, 1975.

and I was given the chance to touch it
it's a small
magnificent piece
about this size
extremely light
and the Pachamama
is the mother of the spacetime
in Quechua
even today
the mother of a spacetime
with a hole to be fertilized
by thought
by thinking
by acting
by planting
itself

to see my own (w)holeness
I come to you
traveling through my own fear
I have to believe
with my ancestors
that **I** am the seed
for the time being
I am the seed
they placed in me
I am the living seed
the seed
that has
two eyes
the word seed
two e's
two eyes
two I's

For the time being
I am alive
I am
the continuing thread
mallki[63]
is the seed in Quechua
mallki
is the ancestor in mythic terms
only the dead
are truly alive
they are
in forever time
in memory
that is
provided
someone
remembers
provided
there is someone
something to remember
it needs other
two eyes
eyes
are the acts looking at us
our own eyes
memory is the chain of resurrection
Charles
Olson
said
memory is the future
because you will
remember in future tense
you will remember

63. Also fruit tree in Quechua.

whatever you did
and others did
and others will do
that is the change
think think
of
the killers
a desperate call for connection
think of
their
memory
think of their memory

the
ethos
being
not a custom
a disposition of a people
like the dictionary says
the ethos being first
seu su
a pronoun
of the third person
referring back to the subject
and to social
group
the social group
as an entity as a whole
the goodness
of it all
the well-being of it all
of the whole
we
ourselves

at stake
the ethos
and this reminds me
of a little film
I saw one day
did you see
it was a film
that showed
through the eye of the microscope
and what it showed
is that even unicellular beings
know what's good for them
when something is about to kill them
they immediately
drive away
away of harm's way
unicellular
beings
know how to do that
how come we don't

The thread of it all
the thread of memory
in Spanish is recordar
as Leslie was saying
to touch again
the heart
in Quechua it is
soncco
hapik
soncco
hapik
amtaña in Aymara is recordar[64]

64. To remember.

amu, el botón de la flor
the bud of the flower
to be empty is not to have a flower within
not to have memory
to have soncco
to have a heart
is to have
the thread of all the plants inside
of you
the Latin cor
the Quechua hapik
soncco hapik
meeting
once more
once again

SEE-ing ourselves
in a CON-tinuum
the CONtinuum
again is
with thread
tenue
tino is a thread only a thread
the force being the stream
of
us
all

y eso sería todo por ahora

singing:
un poquito uhuhuhuhuhuhuhuh
un poquito ah ah ah ah ah ah ah....

un poooo....qui   iiiiiiiiii t ooooooo
un poquito, un poquito, un poquito
uh uh uh uh ....
un po-   qui-   toooo........

shaking seed gourd

Well you know these seeds
are
a kind of seed
that I picked up just off the studio
of the kids
I was visiting
the artists
I was visiting
the other day
I'm sure you've all seen them around
they are from a tree we call algarrobo[65]
I don't know how you call it
in English
but
I wanted to begin
with la sonaja,[66]
because
you know
this is really
the music
of seeds
and although I was supposed to speak
of seeds
ummm, I don't really think I can speak
of seeds
I can tell you

65. Carob or locust tree.
66. Rattle.

a few stories though
about what other people
say
or think of seeds
for example
Nimuendaju[67]
speaking
of what the Guaraní think of seeds
he says:

switching to a more incantatory, rhythmic voice:

"The mbaraká sounds
seem to INvite one
to present oneself
before
the divinity
transporting the dancers into ecstasy
as if the desire of this TIRED race
for its mother
was crying inside of it"[68]
the desire of the seed
crying inside
the sonaja
CRYING inside for the TIRED race
TIRED race
TIRED race
el mate
la calabaza
la lagenaria[69]

67. Anthropologist Curt Nimuendajú, born Curt Unkel in Germany in 1883, studied the Guaraní, as well as other peoples indigenous to Brazil. He died in 1945.
68. Nimuendajú, "Creations Myths," quoted by Lawrence Sullivan in *Icanchu's Drum: An Orientation to Meaning in South American Religions.* NY: Macmillan, 1988.
69. Bottle-shaped seed.

THESE little gourds
that we play that we played
they can only be preserved
if you cultivate them
if you cultivate them
you cannot preserve them
in a seed bank
NO not at all
no way
no way
only through being alive,
they can live
only that
picture that
such a simple thing
aunque no se comía
they didn't eat
the seed
with sounds in them
they went about further
then any other kind of trade
because their real trade
was ecstasy
that's what they wanted to get about
dancing into
EC-stasy
with the help of the little seeds
the seed-spirit
what spirit? come on! it's only breath
it's only breath
it's only breath
the only breath
within the seed itself
the only seed itself

lagenaria
the word is a wound they said
the word is womb
la casa de adentro
la chucha del alma
lo que tienes adentro
guaguita
lo que nadie puede borrar[70]
the word is a womb
she is the disembodied
head image
of a spirit somebody said
what spirit I said again
it's the breath just only
the breath
supernatural beings
they say
supernatural beings
what do you mean
what do you mean
playing it
during rituals
fulfills the destiny
of the human spirit
to sustain
the order of existence
Lawrence
Sullivan
said
that is what he said
that is what he said
sustain the or

70. In English: the house inside / the soul's bed / what you have inside / little one/ what no one can erase.

the ar
coming down
the arm
the order
the right
the spirit
the music of the world
the seed spirits
you know NOTH-ing
the Kariña shaman
says
you know
nothing
but they know
on your behalf
they know
on your behalf
the seeds
are the voices
the seeds
are the voices

And for that reason
I wanted to mention
to you
the Taki Onkoy
the Taki Onkoy
this is an homage
to a man that works
in this university
his name is Thomas Zuidema
I don't know if he's here
or he's not

but he's been writing
quite a bit
about the Taki Onkoy
this is a disease
a dancing disease
that attacked
the Quechua people
the Quechua people
in the 16th century
and these people went dancing about
went dancing about I meant
in the Taki
that is the chant–dance
performed
during the seed
time
this is the dance
for the seeds,
a dance for the seed of the soul
to wake up
it is
one of the forms
of Wanka
a special ritual
and somebody says
a song-love-labor-rite-performance
a concert with the ultimate
harvest
the final
germination
of the LAAst
seed
the terminal
afflictions

of individual
people
beings
and the last cycle
of the Pleiades
the dancing
sickness
of the Pleiades
is the final
round
of cosmic
time
and perhaps
we are Taki
Onkos
all of us
dancing
the music
of the seeds
in the last dance
before the seeds
go away
before too many seeds
go away

As I was coming here
Linda Duke
gave me this
piece of paper

She said
I have a present
for you
look at the present

she says
this from the
Illinois News Gazette

farmers
losing
crop
varieties
as
species
dwindle
dwindle dwindle dwindle ?
Remember that song?

80 percent
of seeds
available a century ago
now extinct
extinct
extinct
extinct
extinct

and now I speak of other forms
of extinction

People wanted to know how this music
of the seeds
how the seeds' song
began for me

it began on a hot
summer
day

I was in Cerro Alegre de Valparaíso
the Cerro Alegre
this was probably because of prostitutes
who knows
but Cerro Alegre
means joyful
joyful hill

I was there
on a hot summer day
I was at the foot
of these native huge
pines
the pines
that sway
in the heat
and suddenly a pine cone
came into my hand
and started to fill my hands
to fool my hands
to gather my hands
around the seeds
somehow
the seeds
started to climb
to be on me
to bother me
to be around me
and I started to
realize
that in this cone
there was a whole universe
a whole forest
in just one little cone

I went about
planting these little seeds
filling up my parents' house
because I was only
a young girl
with little seedlings
and following up their growth
until they were everywhere
and once they were everywhere
I started to speak
to other people
this was Chile
during the Popular Unity times
in the early 70s
probably around '71
and so people
started to come home
to pick up
these little baby trees
that had been growing and were already about
this tall
once they were this tall
they were ready to go into shantytowns
into other places
where they could exist
and so it occurred to me
to propose
to Allende something
that he would call
or I would call
El Banco de Ideas
the Bank of Ideas
so that all kinds of people
from all over Chile

could invent
all kinds
of different things
to help the seeds
to help different ideas
sprout in Chile
Allende thought this was quite
amusing
he thought this was quite
wonderful
quite funny
quite crazy
he said
yes
but Chile is not ready
perhaps by the year 2000 by the year 2000
And once
Linda Duke
and other people here at the Krannert Art Museum
read that story
they probably started thinking
maybe we are in the year 2000
maybe we are about to begin
on behalf of seeds again
I wonder
I wonder
I wonder
in the wondering
in the three W W W
we may begin

I think in a way
what we will do
what we are doing

is a lesson of botany
in reverse
there is no seed
there is no core
only reflections
energy fields
of other
invisible
seeds
the myth says
plants are the teachers
a form
of knowledge
every
living
thing
a form of knowledge
la semilla es la memoria[71]
the encoded memory
the seed is the artwork
of the plant
the little sculpture
salto preparación
todo dice ya
estoy lista para vivir
arriesgarlo todo en el tránsito
antes de llegar
a ser y ceder el paso
a otra semilla[72]
having no ground
they now wish

71. The seed is the memory.
72. Skip prepared-ness / everything says / I'm ready to live / risk everything in transit / before arriving / becoming and yielding / to another seed.

to sprout
in us
having
lost their
ground
to greed
the contrary
seed
by now
they now
want to flower
in dreams
to sprout in gardens
of thought

In virtual reality
somebody said
in a meeting yesterday
as if the World
Wide
Web
the virtual world
of imagination
and the invisible world
of myth
could
come to
meet
Greed
and deed
the seeding
of seeds
now
HOW

we create
the ground
for it
to sprout again
the work to create
grounds within
our own grounds
grounding ourselves
we'll give the seeds
a new ground
Thoreau and Emerson said
the study of nature
and the study
of oneself
are the same
are the same
jardinera ven
decinaban decían
germ, germ, germinaban en mí
decían brotando en mí
sprout in me
sprout in me
brotando la imágen
del imán del gene
del imán del gene

imán del gene[73]
the image
is its own gene
its own gene
perhaps

73. Come gardener / they are say-minating, they said / germ, germ, germinating in me / they said sprouting in me / sprout in me / sprout in me / sprouting from the image / from the gene's magnet / from the gene's magnet // gene's magnet

a thought
is that seeds
had to go
so far away
from the Earth
to begin
to sprout
to have the line
of the poem
go back to the Earth
go back to the Earth
to fertilize
the Earth

turn it off again

this is the last image
that we will see

This is another piece
from the museum
it is a Paracas piece
it is a fragment
as you can see
and I like it because it completely confuses
the art in it

You can see
what it is
it is a piece

of earth
it is a piece of clay
it is a pottery
and it probably is
a seed
it looks like a seed
doesn't it?

it is a seed
again
with eyes
a seed
that is a being
but when you look at it
and you remember the culture
where it comes from
it comes from Paracas
Paracas, Nazca

And you probably have heard
this is a place
where the people
created these writings
or drawings in the desert
that are sooo huge
that you cannot see them
when you are next to them
you have to either
fly above them in a plane
which means 2000 years
after they were created
or you have to climb
on a mountain
and see them

from the distance
and then they become
legible
readable
as images

but this
is just
a clay pot
a piece of earth

please close it down

turn it off

And I wanted
to tell you
another story
about these Nazca lines
these Nazca lines were apparently forgotten
for 2000 years
and uh
people started to discover them
in Perú and come around them and so forth
until an American man
and his wife
his name was Paul Cossock
and his wife Rose[74]
they came to Perú

74. See Vicuña's "Libro Desierto / Desert Book" (trans. R. Alcalá) in *A Book of the Book*, edited by Jerome Rothenberg and Steven Clay. New York: Granary Books, 2000. 286-289.

this was in the 50s
and they came to study
irrigation channels
and they heard
that in the desert of the south coast
of Perú there were these irrigation canals
and so they went there and they looked at them and they said
this is no irrigation canal—not at all—
they went up a mountain and started to look down
and suddenly it was the solstice and they could see that some of the lines align
with the setting sun
and they had a revelation and **[inaudible]**
said for an instant they became like the ancient astronomers priests having an
ecstatic instant watching against the lines
aligned with the earth and their own thoughts ….**[lapse in recording]**

...but the way
I think of them is these lines
in a sense
they ARE irrigation canals
but they are irrigation canals
for the thoughts
and the imagination
of the people
who look at them
both then and now

They are a symbolic
irrigation
a way to speak
to the fertility
of the land.

They are speaking

back to the body
of her
the Pachamama
the mother
of spacetime

People think now
that what people did
with these lines
was DANCE about them
go about
the lines
dancing
and
even today
in the Andes people
go into ecstacy
through dancing
as if the ecstacy
would generate
a form of breath
a form of samay[75]
a form of fertility
for the Earth
as if the stomping
the ground
the rhythm
of the seeds
they are moving
in their hands
and the rhythm
of their thoughts and their bodies
were creating

75. *Samay* in Quechua can mean breath or spirit; it can also mean to rest.

again
a fertility for the soil
for the breath
of the earth
itself

And I wanted to say
it is easy to think
or to say
that these images
of seeds
are beings
are "animistic"
when you say that word
you shut
off
you use
a definition
that shuts
off
the possibility
of seeing them
as carriers
of meanings
of future potentials
I mean
in ancient times people would say that the seeds
the maliki
the ancestor
the dead one
was an oracle
and when you come
to think
of it

the seeds today
perhaps
THEY are the speakers
Perhaps they will speak
more of us

than our own words

Perhaps their visibility
their death will speak more
than ourselves

Coming here
to Champaign
I had a dream
which was to see
the little bit of prairie
left
and I went to see
this little bit
you can see it
you can recognize
the little bit of prairie
probably about THIS big
smaller then the hole
in the Nazca ceramic
smaller than the hole
the prairie left
THINK
of what people
will think of our universities
of all OUR knowledge
put together
if we let the prairie

die
if you let the perfume
the fragrance
the smell
of the waving grasses
if you let that sound
of the grasses
of the grasshoppers
there
When we went about
it was dusk
and the little buds
of Queen Anne Lace
EACH had a grasshopper
in it
I remembered the poem
of the Guaraní people
of the rainforest
They said
that the grasshoppers
they were working
in the formation
of the prairies
they were the workers
the insects
working
creating the prairie
You come down
into the museum
and somewhere
I believe
in the ground floor
you will find the grass spirit
The grass spirit

is a form
of Chinese calligraphy
of course
the grass spirit
but if you go
into somewhere here
you will find
David Monk[76]
who is somewhere
sitting here
I can see his hair waving out there
in the wind of the coldness
of this room
thinking again
let's have the prairie
waving again
so to say goodbye
I will tell you a dream
I had as a girl
this dream
was of a new form of poetry

This form of poetry
was like this:
a mother was walking in the grass
and her children
were walking behind her
so she said to them HUSSHH
and listen
to the sound
of the grass
as we speak
the sound

76. David Monk is an environmentalist working to preserve the prairie ecosystem in Illinois.

of the grass
is the poem
we are writing
together
as we speak

Gracias.

applause and gourd shaking

UNIVERSITY OF MINNESOTA'S RARIG CENTER

APRIL 12, 2001

sky tinted water
minne ha ha
laughing water
los montones del olvido
el Mapocho
el cordón umbilical
a tension
bet
rem & forgett.

el tejido de hoyos
a net of holes
not even shields
can hold such
emptiness

• Luis gómez

el dar vuelta. el poema
Space time
chile polos
en esclavitud 2.244 a consume
slavery

• manquehue

umber site > Del arbol fluye la piel
• Chusquez Quila
Don Alejandro → inner
variant

olvidadoras
"net working", web of life
memory is born at the inter
section
of time/space
el com

- cordón
- corral
- cruz del Sur
- unir los 2
lados
el com
- cloud-net
net working
web of life
• shadow
tejido
de hoyos
luis gómez
N.Y.

el com

the brain evolved in con flict

that's why searching for a common ground

brings social evolution

noema

steps to the quantum

leap

a

pachamuti

events

are

we need to take

a self not self

but a net

a nerve

is not a nerve

but a bundle

of fibers

interconnecting

the nervous

system

utopías organizativas

una idea escrita

en un cajón

a nerve fiber

is a "thread like

process"

an axon or

dendrite

~~Sky tinted Water~~

the plea
sure
of place
the
226 | ~~the~~

of
plea
sure

for
plea
sure

Pleasure
of place
is the
place

Plea
sure of/the
place of/the
plea
sure

Plea
sure
of/the Place

el
poema
Void

of/the
plea
sure

to Plea,
the only
sure sine cura
place.

San Juan.

place : a portion of space
an area with definite or indefinite
boundaries

M.E space, locality fr. O.French fr.
Latin platea broad street, space

fr. Gr.
plateia
fr. fem. platus
broad

flat
plaza

(these broads)

las
desparra
madas

plat - to spread
extended root
pele -
variant form *plad → flat, germanic
flatr O.norse
flett O.E

flan O.F.
flounder O Swedish

L. planta
sole of the foot
plantare
to drive in
with the sole
of the foot

(the dagger)

(obscure origin
L. spatium + space, distance.)

clan

Place
an
empty
expanse

WOODLAND PATTERN BOOK CENTER

MINNESOTA, SEPTEMBER 29, 2001[77]

AHHHHH
UHHHHHH
AHHH hhhhhhhh haaa haaa haaaa haaaaa
hhaaa hhhhaaa

hhhheeeh heeeh eheheeeeh

Canoas
de luz

La vida viaja en canoas de luz
el cosmos vacío insemina la tierra
la madre y la hija
jueee-gan a hilar
suuuube el cor-don
umbiiiiilica nave
haaablen
carencias
luuuz del sonar
el hilo sueña el lenguaje
el habla respoooonde-luz
respoonde luz

la madre teje un telar
la niña sus pies
de las hebras de la inmensidad

---

77. Transcribed from an audio recording.

el polvo
danzando
en un rayo de luz
el polvo tan santo en un rayo de luz

Weaving
is the birth
of light
Lezama Lima
says

Weaving is the birth
of light he says
and others say
DNA is a life
is a light
emitting thread
each living cell
emitting light
light
light
light
life
travels
in canoes
of light
the empty cosmos
emits a murmur

into a

mother

and daughter
plaaay
playyyy
at something
the cord

umbilical
vessel
umbi navi
ubi nuvi
umbi

patterns of speech

sound of light
the thread
dreeeeaaams

dreams
of language
speech
responds
in light

I don't see a thing huh

with or without

But just to make sure

It's dark in the desert night

It's dark in the desert night

And they are dancing the lines
dancing the lines
walking the well into life
walking the well into life
becoming the well
dancing the line the well lines
becoming the well
entering into well
entering well
being well
well come
come
come
come
come on
come one well
come union well
come on come on come on well
well dance while they dance
dance a line
dance all night
rest all night

And speaking of dance in the desert
dance in the desert light

You want to know about the grammar of dance?
This is what they are doing
this is the desert at night
the desert at night
with huuuge lines
drawn for the night sky to see
llamacñawin
llamacñawin
These are the eyes of the llama at the foot of the Southern Cross constellation
these are the eyes in the **[inaudible]**[78]
constellation of light they say
in the constellation grammar of the North
in the South is llamacñawin
the eyes of the llama watching down
into the desert
people are coming
their trance to irrigate the dance
irrigate the land
irrigate the dânce
the breath of the dance
they're dancing their lines
and speaking of Nazca

Nazca the de sert night **almost a whisper**

sings:

Libro oxidado[79]
Librooooo oxiidaado
Textoos bailadooss bailados

---

78. The eyes are probably a reference to the Alpha and Beta Centauri.
79. A variation of "Libro Desierto / Desert Book," which appears in *A Book of the Book*.

y abandonaados
y despediii-dos

Ahhhh-xidized book
texts abandoned
book of nothing
dust and departure
book of time and stone
shifting
book of breath
here I go
I write with wind
oxidizing dust
I write with breeze
dyeing the stone
I write with booody
dancing the mud
I write with gestures cross
and tem temporal crossing
my hide of skin
the earth inscribed
who
reads
the signs?

the pampas tattooed
the red on the thigh
the trace erased
who
reads
the
signs?

nocturnal sky

a stellar dust
the she in desert dried dustless
foooountainhead
daaaance
fountainhead
haaand
she tattoo
tattooing her body
with stars
the clit the clit
cleee-toris she doesn't want to say
clit
clit
she's saying
a door budding its key
the center and border
pleasure spring
finding I found her
marking her signs
the earth her [inaudible]

not earth

not body

a mark
clit growing out
of time
in [inaudible] *signs*

sings:

manan-manan-aaaa-manantial ...[80]
[inaudible]

When people come
to the Nazca lines
they never wonder
of the ancient
names
that disappeared in the desert
together with the dancers
and some names remain in the land
the little town
that still remains alive after everything else is called
is called Cahuachi
CA HUA Chi
It means
make them see

the desert lines
to make them see

who will see

the night sky

who will

see

make them see

---

80. *Manantial* means spring or source.

CAA HUA Chi
CAA HUA Chi

papers rustling

About a book in the desert
A desert book they say
A book for the space within words
A book is a space
for the invisible tension
be-tweeeen words

betweeen words

Empecé coleccionando pequeñas conchas de perla[81]
fragmentadas y hechas polvillo
me costó mucho
reunir
los pedacitos de aire entre ellas
obtuve cerca de dos piezas
llenas de conchas
llenas de aire entre ellas
conchas azules y verde negras
sin que nunca se repitiera
un aire
ni una forma
ni un pedacito
entre ellaaas
entre concha y concha

81. "Empecé coleccionando..." to "las humedecía" is a variation of the poem "Nácar," which was first published in *Saboramí*. Devon, England: Beau Geste Press, 1973.

no es lo que tu estás pensando
la concha es justo lo que estás pensando entre ellas
todas estaban durmiendo
una blanca vaguedad
las humedecía
las humedecía
las humedecía

in repsonse to a baby murmuring:

yeeaaahhh

Mother of Pearl[82]

I started
I started
I didn't
I started I started
collecting tiny
nacre
shells
fragmented AND turning
into duSSSt
duSSSt
gathering BITS of air
BITS of air
between them
was tough
tough

I was able to fill
twooo roooooms
of aaair in betweeeen the shells

82. "Mother of Pearl" to "dampened them" is a variation of my translation of "Nácar," which appeared in *Open City* 14 (Winter 2001-2002): 153.

blue ones and dark green
without repeating one air
one form
one small bead of aiiir

all were weeping
all were sleeping

a white white white
vah-gue-ness
vagueness
vah vagueness
dampened them

[inaudible] *tiempo*
desertores de su propia fragilidad
lo único vivo en ellos
es lo que no morirá
porque los nutre sin sostenerlos
los sustentan traspasándalos
deshaciéndolos

Un libro de no-cuerpos
un libro de cuerpos
con pelos
y órganos tejidos
un libro móvil que se trastoca en las manos
y responde
a los pensamientos

de su co autor
que lo toca y pregunta afectando su composición
LIBRO viviente
que estás ahi viviendo
y sintiendo a medida
que hablamos
tu
y yo[83]

Seed me now[84]
seed me now
seed YOU later

a sound is the seed of the universe
the
sound
said
a seed is the word of the earth
the
earth
said
they didn't say the word
they didn't say ANY of that
geometric vulva
geometric vulva they said
spatial vessel

---

83. From "Tiempo" to "tu y yo": time / deserters of their own fragility / the only thing alive in them is what will not die / because it nourishes them more than sustenance / sustains them piercing / dissolving them. // A book of no-bodies / a book of bodies / with hair / and organs tissues / a mobile book that transforms in the hands / and responds to the thoughts of its co-author // who touches it and asks transforming its composition / living book / there alive / and listening while / you and I / speak.

84. Beginning with "Seed me now," to the end of the performance, is a variation of the poem "Se Mi Ya" in translation. A recording of this translation can also be found on the CD included in *Rattapallax* 9 (2003). The Spanish original was published in the catalog for "Semi Ya," an art installation and exhibit of seed sculptures at the Galeria Gabriela Mistral in Santiago, Chile (2000).

waiting to bud
gather many seeds
I said
in one place
gather them in order to gaze
and love the seeeeds

only one
collective gesture
of love
could stop destruction
the felling and burning of moisture

of moisture
of moist breath

the poet's botany
a table to hear
and touch
seeds
lace of stick
quisca wax

star and torch
echo of the north
patahua POTbelly
and tree barbed lily
tree rhododendron
little coconut
with three
post
unisex flower
strangled strangled
smooth trunked palm tree

and what about these little vine weavers
what
about
what about
them

empty patahua
writing in the air
quipu I seed
the seed is the thread
the thread is the seed
the [inaudible] *is the seed*
where
are
they?

silence

Yesterday
we were gathered here

Some of you were here last night weren't you?
Ya.

And we were speaking about the Fates, remember? And so today in the workshop. Let's see. Let's see if I can see the person. Yeah. Somebody brought—but she isn't here now. No. Somebody brought another book on the Fates. So—It was you! Oh! How wonderful! So. Oh. Good, good, good. Because I seem to remember that it was somebody else because I get in a state peculiar and I don't remember things right.

audience member says: "I was someone else this morning."

Oh, I see. So we're together in this. That's good, that's wonderful. So, this was meant for you, you know. So I'm going to do this this for you. And this happened through an accident, and I told the story last night so those who heard it will hear a transformed repetition now.

And I had invited
this large group of people
to come and dance with me by the river
and as it turned out only three women showed up
And so once I saw
them
dancing with the threads
I started to think that they were the Fates
all over again
And for the Fates
are in three names
and
I will tell you
so that you can make more fun of it
the three names
of the Fates
this is in Greek:
one
is
called

Clotho
and Clotho she's the mother of the cloth
that we wear
It is actually exactly the same
word
so in reality the cloth that we wear
is not at all cloth
this is only an illusion.
What it is, according to this myth
is that the cloth is your time here
so the cloth is really your life
and the way you are living it
so this is Clotho
the spinner
of
fate
and your fate is your cloth
think of that
You know?
Then comes
the woman that's called
Lachesis
hmmm
Lachesis is the one that
allots
to each one
a portion.
And you should know
that the word
name
also means portion
So
each
one

of
our
names
is a portion of the total name
the name that's composed of all names
and nouns
And the last of them,
this is the terrible one
this is AAAtropos
you know tropos
tropos is the movement
so atropos is the one
that won't move
A—a
is of course the negation
the one that won't move
the inflexible one
the one that cuts the thread
no matter what.
And did you know that now
with all this DNA research
they have found that we have a thread inside
our genes that's called the telómeros.
Do you know
about this?
And the telómeros
is cut
before
we're born
through a genetic message
so the Greeks
were onto something
weren't they?

audience laughter

The one that cuts

So here
I am turning around
the Fates

Perdonen Señores

And this is something that's very nice
This, um,
when you try to find
the places
where in myth
in Greek myth
or in stories that started to be written
by the Greeks themselves
about this myth
it is often called the "Legend of Er"
Er
I don't know how the Greeks
pronounced er:
EEE-AHRR
and I like that very much
because it's the root of error
error[85]
so it's like perhaps it's all
an error, and it would be wonderful
to think
we are an error — **audience laughter**
And the Muslims
you know, they say
that errors

85. "Error," which shares the same spelling and meaning in both languages, is pronounced first in English, then in Spanish.

are really offerings

I like that

So
it
says[86]:

[inaudible] *y cloto lachesis atropos*
spinning life
and death

... fate
but fate is not the force

fate is not the force
that predetermines events
as the dictionary says
fate is to speak
and you fate yourself as you speak
as you name the name
a turn of phrase becoming blood
your destiny
to hit the mark
destiny
it really means
hit the mark
and they came to a mysterious place the myth says
at which
there were

---

86. This "introduction" is followed by a variation of the poem "Er," which, Vicuña notes, "intertwines different translations of 'The Fable of Er,' an orphic myth appearing in *The Iliad*, *The Odyssey*, and Plato's *The Republic*" (*cloud-net.* New York: Art in General, 1999: 34-38, 95).

two chasms
two holes it says
two heavenly openings
two earthly openings
two again
the number two
by one
each pair
souls departed
and by one the other came back
both of them moving like this
and there in that
in ter me diate space
it was the South Finger Pier
in Lower Manhattan
a cool summer night
in that between-ness
they were told
YOU
will be the messenger
YOU will be the messenger
of what YOU see

dancing and balancing the thread
in the air bladers pass by
waving their blades
weavers weaving their waves
after
seven days
they came to a shaft
of light

like a column standing through the whole heaven and earth
a beam of light they said

like a child dancing in the dust
and here
translators disagree
a series of circles surrounded the shaft
eight of them they said
the whorl of the spindle
and each of them
a siren
hummmed
a note
hummmmmmedanote
el cronos de cuerda
el hilo de voz
All notes creating one
haaar
mooo
ny

all notes turning a sound
on which revoluuuution turns
revolution turns
depends
I said
revolution
on turn
in turn
depends harmos being
a joining
a harm
a harm
turning into
har
har
har

mony
an agreeee
ment
a woman angry at the thread
caught in her bike
said
is this a booby trap

only your mind
the booby trap

the girls thought

as she threw the weave into the river
dark as the sea
the thread
pulsating and throbbing
a heart
in the sea

and in the extremity of it
three girls
pushed
to the edge
by the force of the spin
puuushed
pushed to the spin
puuushed
pushed to the limit
spinning of necessity
three
girls
singing
at

once
of the present future and past
spinner allotment
on
never
turn
back
never
turn
back
each
one
a
portion
a fragment
of ourselves
a shaft
of light
a thread
of light
sobbing
sobbing
in the sea

I cannot help but think of the things that happened when we were doing that dance and this is again for the people who saw the film last night. In this dance, we were dancing at the pier, a few yards, not a few yards, I should say, like ten blocks away from the World Trade Center. And so for now for me it's impossible to read this, and not see each time the two shafts of light. You know. This is what happened. You know the towers disappeared and they became this white light going up and I didn't realize of course any of this but poetry has this bad -abit. Or how do you pronounce –Hh-abit. Hmm? Of saying things before they happen. You know? It's a scary thing. And you try not to but in any case it's not up to you, it's up to something else. And so em, I want to read you some poems that were written—here it says '97, so that I hope it must be true. And one of them is a very sad story, and at a few blocks from my place—actually, only a block and a half, this story actually happened. An Ecuadorian me-grant, mi-grant worker was digging a hole for Con Edison, hmmm and apparently he felt very tired, and he took a little nap at the end of the hole, and one of this co-workers came with this huge machine with tons of rubble, and nobody took notice of the little migrant worker

sleeping
under and threw all the rubble
on top of him
nobody noticed
that he had been gone
nobody
none of his co-workers
missed him
they closed the hole
put cement on it
night came
and he was missed at home by his brother
And his brother
came to the workplace and said:
Where is my brother Luis?
Your brother Luis? Nobody even remembered him
And this is very telling
because this is like our position
the position of the little dark ones
Nobody even notices

whether we are
or we are not
there
And this man, the brother,
insisted: He's here in this hole **[tapping the lectern]**
And they fought him and said no, no he's not
He probably disappeared
He went somewhere else
If he was here we don't remember
Denying the whole thing
Until he pressed, he pressed, he pressed, and finally they opened the hole and there it was:
Luis, crushed, like this

Of course, he was dead

So this poem is in memoriam for Luis[87]

Escoooombro y olvido
sue-ño malherido
el enterrado vivo
el hombre deshecho
sin cuerpo ni abrigo
viajaaando en el ruido
el hoooombre deshecho
viajaaaando enel ruido

Forgotten rubble
wounded dream you are

87. Followed by a version of "Luis Gómez" (translation by R. Alcalá), which appeared in *XCP: Cross Cultural Poetics* 8, "Authenticating (Dis)Location / (Dis)Locating Authenticity." College of St. Catherine-Minneapolis, 2001: 52-53.

discarded alive
man undone
no body
no warmth
noise in transit
discarded man
undone you are

And then the last poem in this sequence is inspired by a confluence of three things.

In Chile, before the Spaniards came there were many peoples who spoke many languages. And one of them was the Mapuche people—this is in the south of Chile where we have something we call La Selva Fría, which is the cold rainforest—it's extremely cool. And it's extremely misty with these huge immense magnificent trees, so it's a completely different idea of the rainforest, a rainforest where it is eternally cool. Nevertheless, the Mapuche who lived there had this custom which is that they would get up every day everybody in the community—old people, babies, everybody would get up at 4 a.m. in the morning no matter how cold it was, and they would all walk to the waterfall and they would all bathe
in the cold waterfall. So when the white people arrived they ask—well, why do you do that? And they said: to warm up. **audience laughs**

Ok, so I am flying and arriving at Buffalo. You've been to Buffalo, you know? So you know that if you come to Buffalo on a clear day you see two waterfalls. Have you had this experience? You see one waterfall that's going up and one waterfall that's going down

Have you seen that?
Have you?

And this is the mist the mist is so thick
and so white that it condenses as an upside-down
waterfall you know
So this is for that waterfall

Let's see

[sings]

Laaaavaaan-do[88]
Laaaavaaan-do
Laaaaaaa laaaaavando
Lavandoooo van do
Lavandan lavando lavando lavando
lavandan...

...lavándolo en una falsa cascada...

...melinkooo la-uen...
melinkoo lauen

cascada..

caaaa caaa ... [inaudible]

Fake Waterfall

Washing a tangled thread
washing a tangled thread
in a fake
waterfall

88. This sung segment is a variation of the poem "Falsa cascada." What follows is a variation of "Fake Waterfall," its translation. Poem and translation appear in *XCP: Cross Cultural Poetics* 8, 50-51.

melinko lauen
entering the waterfall's mist
they drank
heavvvy drops
melinko la-uen
upside down vowel
ascending dew
world inside out
melinkkkooo
lauen
melinkhooo
la-uen

And this one last thing I forgot to tell which is in the word melinko lauen—that is Mapuche for the mist around the waterfall, and the concept is that it is not the waterfall that's healing but it's the mist that flies away, and in each one of the drops of the mist the world is turning itself inside-out upside-down. And it is in that turning the world upside-down that the healing is. So perhaps that is our offering for the towers that is going up that is going up. Is going up. Not down.

And with that thought let's hope for peace.

Okay that would be all.
Okay thanks.

applause

What do you think? It's about right. Yes, it is. Isn't it? Too short or too long?

One more? **applause**

Gracias, let's see.
Which one should I do?

Well, this is our last book. This is a dirty book. It's usually everything that I do is quite dirty. This is inspired by the dirtiest poem in the book and I give you that because you need something dirty to shake up. And the way this happened—this is the work of a Catalonian painter, his name is Manel Lledós and he came to me and he said why don't we do a book where you will do the poems and I will do the painting based on your poems, so I said okay and I brought together these few little poems, and he came up with this and with this, and another one that is lost. **[holding up the book]** See?

So, okay the concept of this book is called El Templo.[89] It is one of those impossible things to translate because templo, you know, temple, the concept of temple and the concept of time are actually one. So it begins with Little Nemo. Do you remember Little Nemo? You do? Isn't that great? Well, okay. **laughter**

Little Nemo says:
bring them to time

time from tem, to cut
bring them to temple I say
space set aside
for contemplation
they say
el templo es el tiempo

---

89. *El Templo.* Translated by Rosa Alcalá, with paintings by Manel Lledós. New York: Situations Press, 2000.

dawn and daybreak
time before death birth
a cut thread
the moon who is our mother
she made day into living beings
[inaudible] night says

el templo es el día y orar es diamar estar en el
sabién do lo
day is temple
day in prayer
knowing day
temple day
to divine
they say
in Maya, one word ki'j means day
k'ijlabal means to pray
in other words to love the day
and ki'jloxic actually means
to divine
to divine is being in the day
knowing
knowing the day

la herida es un ojo
sangra la mirada
la sed
es la vida misma
del manantial
vast and empty
the heart
is heaven
they say

empty only a saying
to fill
with pleasure[90]

the Mayas

say
that one of the names
of God
is heart of heaven
heart of earth

but do you know what they mean?
they don't really mean that there is someone
someone
called a god
or someone called a heart
but there is a meeting place
a meeting place
called [inaudible]
—that is the heart—
not a god not us
but a meeting point
for all
that is called [inaudible]

And this is the dirty one and this will truly be the last.
And this is based again on the Nazca and to [inaudible] with the first—the poem I was reading you about desert. And that poem is inspired by a little sculpture, a ceramic of a woman probably done by a woman, where this woman is naked with her body completely tattooed by stars and images of the cosmos and then she has her legs open like that and her clitoris sprouting

90. In this section, Vicuña reads poems and translations from *El Templo*.

out, sprouting up—how could you say?—what would be the preposition? You know, in any case, it's budding as her guiding light. This is my interpretation. **laughter**

So, of course, you will never find this interpretation in anthropology or archaeology. And so this is for the woman who created that ceramic piece and probably those women who wrote those huge lines in the desert, which for me are a book.

And so, this is for her.

Nazca

torna la mano
el gozo feroz
el giro pensante de otro rumor
el cuerpo es la tierra

el plano escultor
el clitoris manda
el acto es la estrella
fertilizar
rodando espiral
rodando
espiral

Nazca

hand spinning

wild pleasure
turn thinking
another thought
body as earth
sculpting plane
clitoris sends
the act star
fertile
spiral
rise

applause

THE POETRY PROJECT AT ST. MARK'S CHURCH
NEW YORK, NY, MAY 15, 2002[91]

[*Introduction*]

silence

YA bolito
YA bolito bo liiitttooo…
booo boo oooo
hilito hilito
tíralo pa ca
tira lo pa ya
hilito hilitoooooOO
mama mama
pásame el hilitooo
cuál hilito CUAL
ese que tienes en la bocaaa…
baba baba baba
eeee
mmmmhhh aaaaa AH

hmmm

that was my mamá she would always put the thread in her mouth
MIJITA VENGA PARA CA laughter
DONDE PUSO LA COSA ..

that's for herrrrrr

---

91. Transcribed from an audio recording. A fragment of this transcript was published in *The Literary Review*: "Global New York," 46.2 (2003): 325-329.

para mamáăá .... [vocables]

hmmm

do you know there's a little house in here

it's good for hiding

don't get scared
I'm not going to do this

She sings:

aaaaalba aaaalbaaaa
aalllbaaaa aalllbaaaa
alba albaaaa aaa a....

a a a
alba saliva
el in—stan
time bending tongue
entwine entwine
the between

[inaudible]

madre
madre del habla
imán del gen
palabra estrella
palabra estrella
mother of time
maaaa maaa maaa maaa
el signo no es

si no
si no
si no
in sinua in sinua
insinua tion
de la nuve la nave
nuve nave
nuve nave
nuve nave-gation
na na na na na na na na
the nuance
nuance of words
the mist
the mist
to go go through

[inaudible]
the space between
between between
between words

imán del cruzar

cros-sing magnet
responde
responde
[unintelligible]
cuál es
cuál es
cuál es nuestra verdad
por qué estamos aquí
por qué
por qué
the I

the I
the I
is the light
del entremedio

responde [inaudible]

you respond

corazón
corazón
del aquí

why are we here
why are we here

[unintelligible]

turning pages

changed heart

the eeem i grant

changed heart

the eem i grant granting me life
un cre er en el cor
changing the heart of the
e e earth
la [inaudible] *del*
llevo

llevo
llevo
lle vo mi ser del futuro
re ci pro cate re ci pro cate
gramaticar
gramaticar....
Relate **[reading]**

córtala!.. [from singing to chanting]

ecstacy el instan...[92]
[applause]

Now we are going to change.

Last night I was a little sick

and they were watching Ali[93]
they were watching, I said
did you notice that? hmmm
They. Who was that?
All my Mes
All my Cecilias
you know
Lying
sick
in
bed watching Ali

92. Vicuña continues to sing a variation of *Instan* in its entirety (Berkeley: Kelsey St. Press, 2002). I've transcribed only the first few minutes.
93. Vicuña is referring to the 2001 film about Muhammad Ali.

Do you remember Ali?
The little dancing feet?
Do you remember him?
I remember we were in Santiago watching him
all of us gathered
hundreds of people
gathered just to watch
one little TV set
this was the original
TV
set
And was there
We was there
watching Ali
the little dancing feet
The unboxing boxer
The unhitting hitter
The undoer doing
My GO——D
And when he said
IIIII am pret-ty,
we felt
WE were pretty
When he said I am black
we felt we are black
It was a shock
to come to the U.S.
and realize that we were not black
after all — **audience laughter**
hmmm

I wonder who narrowed it down — **audience laughter**

We were him certainly

that's for sure
And now I wanted to tell you this story
that's around the Internet
I've no idea whether this is true or not
this is what the Web does:
it undoes the web
doesn't it?

A message came
it says Guaicaipuro Cuatemoc[94]
had been speaking to the European
Community
on February the 8th
19
sorry
18
sorry
002.

He said
UsUUUra[95]
brothers
YOU
who ask
us to pay you
our debt
YOU are asking
to pay YOU our debt
in reality
I
loaned

94. According to information and transcriptions circulating on the Internet, Cacique Guaicaipuro Cuatemoc addressed the Heads of State of the European Community on February 8, 2002.
95. *Usura*: usury

you
millions and millions and million and
ME ME ME ME ME
ME-LEE-YONS
of gooold and silver
as a friendly gesture of the Americas
towards the development of Europe
this was our "Marshalltesuma plan" audience laughter
plan for the reconstruction
of the barbaric Europe
Poor them
But it failed—look audience laughter

In its irrational
capitalistic
ways
they are still at it.
Europe always wants more
they need
more
More
more from us
But time has come for Eur Eur
I can't even say it—
Eu You You You Your
Your-UP.
To return
to us
To return to us
the gold and silver
we so
generously
loooooaned
We ask you

to now sign
a letter of inn-tent
as a way to discipline YOU.

And then I thought
of this Ino Moxo[96]
This Ino Moxo is a
black panther
It's impossible
It is not a black panther
It's a person
becoming
a black panther
How can it be?
There are no black panthers
in the Amazon
and this is an
Amazon man
He says "Cuando pienso en Fitzcarraldo
y en sus mercenarios
cuando pienso que esos genocidas
eran hombres
me dan ganas

96. Peruvian poet César Calvo interviewed the Amawaka shaman Ino Moxo, which means "black panther," in the 1970s, and wrote a memoir based on his experience: *Las tres mitades de Ino Moxo.* Iquito, Perú: Talleres Editorial Gráfica Labor, 1981. See also *The Three Halves of Ino Moxo: Teachings of the Wizard of the Upper Amazon,* Trans. Kenneth Symington. Rochester, VT: Inner Traditions, Intl., 1995.

de nacionalizarme
cuuu le bra"
I don't know how to do this

but this is Ino Moxo

and he's saying
when I'm thinking of Fitzcarraldo
and his mercenaries
when I think
that those people
committing genocide
that they were people
that they were people
I want to nationalize myself
into a snake

hmmm

That's César Calvo.
Do you know
César Calvo?

He was a Peruvian poet
going to the forest
to drink this little tea
that makes you a little crazy

To drink the sacred little tea
But when you go hear
what he has to say
it's the same I feel
when watching TV here
it's
exactly
the same

I go into this screen
in ecstasy
watching the commercials
MY GO-o-o-D

You know

Wow
These lights
How they glide
How they move
How they
do
that

The shamans
down there
say that that's the way
to see the MaaDness
of the place—
It's not quite true.

Mundo fronterado
in voluto de sierpe negra
y blanca
Vida hora
en tu revés
línea de muerto
línea de vivo
en tus in-STAN-tes

They call
the mother of sound
the mother of voice in the ear
the ayawaskAAA
The thread of the dead
is speaking alive

when you hear them
they say
"El primer hombre
no era hombre
era mujer."

The first man
was not a man
was a woman—
didn't you see that?
Suenan los pasos,
they say

and when I go outside every morning
I go greet the sun
because my place here is dark
dark as a cave
I go down to the street
I open the door
and let the sun in
and I watch the shadows pass by
on Hudson Street
these shadows
are just as it says in the poem
In the poem it says
the shadow
is from the animal

you used to be
the shadow
is from the one
you will be
The shadow is not from you
from them
from the one who passes,
it's not a shadow at all
it is the sound
of a shadow
It is the shadow
of the sound

"apu miski yawar
poderosa sangre dulce
qespichiway yawar
apareame con el cristal
auqay kuna manta
líbrame de mis enemigos"[97]

When Guaicaipuro Cuatemoc began he started by saying
here we are
in
the
encounter
he didn't say that word
he didn't say that word
what he meant is

---

97. Ino Moxo, cited in Calvo, 123.

here we are to counter
each other in the encounter
to balance complement
each
other
to do it to do it
to one another
to one another

And then I was thinking
I was thinking
I didn't want to do
this
for
you
but in a way
it is irresistible
not to do it

You know that when September 11th came
OUR September 11th
I mean

back in 1973[98]

we went into like
a 10-year
mourning
The words have fallen
apart
from us
They had fallen apart
from each other

---

98. The Chilean military coup occurred on September 11, 1973.

The word "ma"
seemed faaaar away
The EM away from the AH
MA
MA
fallen
into the sea

And now with THIS September 11th
here
it's the opposite way
noooo
silence
noooo
distance
no pulling
apart
it feels
like we are narrowly escaping
a next
one

WHERE is that silence
between words?

WHERE
has it gone?

The pax
the peaks
the peace
movement
Where is it?

I remember dreaming
dreaming the first weeks
I came to New York
there was this weeehhh
there was this weeeehhh
there was this HUGE demonstration

Do you remember that?
No Nukes
the whole city
being walked
by no nuking people

do you remember that?

anger is a constellation they say
for removing of shackles
they say
fear is for de-fense
they say

de-fense
de-fence

larva ...[unintelligible]
excavando inflamando
awful memories being tracked
tracked
over and over again
haciendo canalitos canalitos
channels
overstepped
deeper and deeper
grooves in your mind

that's toxic
they say
it leaves a scar
they say
they say a scar
in your mind
we think by feeling
that's why talk works
because it changes the physical train
train?
brain?
the phEEE-sical
brain?

We don't see light
we see WITH light
they say

Soon
ultra thin
sails
will catch the wiiind of light
beams grouped
in bundles
of four will begin
to sing
to sound
sing sing
word association rapid shifts
of attention
they say
ungrammatical strings
and inner music
move like threads

26 pearls in complementary
strand
template they say
all reversed for you to speak

link
link
link please
link my struggles
no
it says
my string

all that was on TV

I heard it on TV

you don't believe do you

I don't either but it's true

And then I wanted to tell you

after your September 11th
which is also my second September 11th
I decided to go to BA
that's Buenos Aires
to take a little refuge
look at the refuge I picked, huh

I was there
I was there

And even few weeks
before the whole thing started
I was scribbling down
these notes

these notes
that were perhaps
in everybody's minds

about the deuda –
you know what the deuda is

the deuda is the debt
the so-called debt
if you go now to the Drawing Center
you will find a little scrap
of paper
that Ellsworth Kelly
took
to make a little drawing
in it
you will see
a little ad from the New York Times
it says:
"Argentina says it's going to pay the debt" (1959) **laughter**

la deudita la deu-dita
if you open the word deu-DA in Spanish
it becomes de uuuuuuuuuuuuuuuuuuuuuuuuuuuuuuuuuuuuuuuuuuuuuuuuu
uuuuuuuuuuuuuuuuuuuuuu
DA

de from
UUU
dAAA
give
you can also read it in portuñol
that's the future language of South America

and it becomes
god gives
deu-da

turn around the U
in a U turn
turned inside out
the UUUUUUUUUUUUUUUUUUUUUUUUUUUUUUUUUUUUUU
UUUUUUUUUUUU

You know in South America
especially in the Andes
when somebody likes you
he doesn't say I like you
the person says
I AM you
if they want to vote for you in a campaign they say
I AM Bush

imagine that

they say I AM el mundial
for the soccer game
they say I AM
el mundial

corriente del con

cada uno se convierte en su contrario
y vuelta a empezar
escrituritas
que hacen vivir
estas dos grietas en la frente
sombras de un árbol en la cara
rastros de un beeeso
pudriéndose en la piel

current of con
the con becomes its contrary
and begins all over again
WRITING
WRITING that gives you life
these
little
grooves
I don't know how to say that

I'm translating for you on the spot
these little grooves on my forehead
these are my
TV channels
I watch astonished
astonished at what I see
sombras de un árbol
the shade of a tree
in your skin
that's la escriturita
the little writing
rastros
the remains of the kiss
already rotten on your cheek
that's the writing

on the wall

arrugas del desvelo
arruguitas
unos días

van para adelante
otros para tras
para dónde se irán
veo veo
qué ves
él es no es del estar
un tejido de huecos
temblando al pasar
my, how could I do that?

that's all

PIEROGI ART GALLERY

BROOKLYN, NEW YORK, NY, SEPTEMBER 12, 2002[99]

I don't know about you
but for me it was very hard
to come here
because of yesterday
and today.

I tried to go to the subway
and I see all the papers
displayed in the newstands
this image of a key hole
and all the people inside
the key hole
what are they doing
crying inside the key hole?

may be may be
their pain
inside the key hole
will let them see
into other pains
other sorrows
in the other September 11s
of the world
the forgotten September 11s
of the world.

but no,
today at 8:00, perhaps

---

99. This is Vicuña's reconstruction of her performance notes, and of how the notes might have been performed. There is no recording.

you were listening
perhaps you heard
apparently we are going
to war
        wawawawawawawawa (**loud lament**)

who is this
        we we we we
in Colombia
the wewe
is your prick
el pico, dick

wawawawa

                war?

Con cha
cunt má

madre del tiempo

con cha

....

(Note: "the key hole" image was an aerial photo of the ramp built for the relatives of the victims to descend into the hole of the WTC towers, to make their offerings on the anniversary of September 11, 2001.)

(En la misma carpeta está esta variante. ¿cuál de las dos leí? o hice una mezcla de los dos en el quasar? no lo recuerdo.)[100]

---

100. In the same folder is this version, but which one did I read? Or did I combine the two into a

“There is no way to peace
Peace is the way”
A.J. Muste

They descended
this ramp
oblique ramp
into the sound
watering sound
of the dead
the dead names
el ruego
es el riego
the watering
sound
el ruego
es el riego
water of life
descending
the ramp.

The towers became the watering hole for the sound of the names.

Tercera variante:

They descended
this ramp
oblique ramp
into the sound

---

quasar? I can’t remember. (Vicuña’s footnote)

of their
names
el ruego
es el riego
pensé
the watering
hole.

"The Pit"

it says & you see a key hole

may be their pain will help them ~~to~~ see

other people's pain

People crying inside a key hole, & you think

pain coming fr Am. planes

as in "Am. planes"

other Sept 11's

.. forgotten Sept 11'

like our own

when pain came fr. planes

shall I say more?

"not in our name" they said

"we will not let them" bomb others

" in our name ..

transformed into a watering hole

they descended this ramp

oblique ramp

into the sound

of their names

el ruego es el riego

pensé

agua el llorar

watering hole

Their names becoming the watering hole

the pit transformed into a watering hole

LISTENING: RESPONDING TO VICUÑA'S PERFORMANCES

HANDSPUN SYLLABLES / HANDWOVEN WORDS: HALLWALLS CONTEMPORARY ARTS CENTER BUFFALO, NY, SEPTEMBER 27, 1998[101]

Dennis Tedlock

A shaft of light strikes the white cloud at the front of the dark room. In the back of the room a woman's voice makes strings of syllables.

The woman walks forward, follows a thread, enters the edge of the light. She holds something between her open hands, palms facing each other.

Threads pass back and forth between her hands, her fingers make a loom. She reads the threads for syllables. Each sound repeats and repeats before another sound replaces it. No words appear among the syllables, not yet.

The woman arrives at the front of the room, turns, and parts the cloud with her hands. It has a microphone inside it. Her first words are those of her first language. Buenas noches she says, she is speaking to us at night. Buenos días she says, weaving is the birth of light. The light of the hand.

Back and forth her weft passes from one language to another: Spanish, English, Latin, Greek, Quechua, Quiché Maya, English, Spanish. She stops to unravel a word here and there, exposing its roots, touching it with her tongue, feeling its fibers with her fingers. Never once does she use the word "web."

I hope I'm quoting my memory right, she says. In Maya day is a noun, q'ij, but it is also a verb, q'ijila, "to day." To day is to pray.

Do you hear me? she asks, she speaks just loudly enough to be heard, just softly enough to make us lean forward to get every word.

---

101. Although Dennis Tedlock was in attendance the night of the performance, this is his response to the videotaped performance.

In the Andes people say an unspun thread contains the power of the cosmos. In Africa they say every day of a person's life is lived in preparation to be an ancestor. Acts are descriptions, a writing in real time. She rearranges the threads on her fingers.

She speaks in syllables again, reading her threads. These are the sounds of a word a woman is not supposed to speak, she says. You could feel it in the thunderstorm that came this morning.

At Naropa that summer we went high enough in the mountains to reach the snow. Then we came down and did a reading in a tent on a lawn. A cloud came over the tent with lightning and thunder, rain came down in big drops. The canvas was pounded by countless syllables. Their sounds remain in the woman's memory.

Buffalo is a cloud city, she says. Manhattan is full of holes. Holes made by fountains from broken water mains, and holes where water disappears. Luis Gómez, a construction worker, was eating his lunch when a machine dumped rubble on top of him. No one noticed. Later, when they removed the rubble, they found a hole, and inside the hole was his little body. He was an illegal alien.

Writing is a sensorial disorder, she says, arranging her threads. Writing wants to be three-dimensional. Like the khipu. In Buenos Aires she dreamed of a street with threads floating over it, waving from the buildings. The next day she found herself in that very street. Women had strung it with threads, and hanging from the threads were photographs of los desaparecidos.

She leafs through a book with thick pages, looking for a poem. The signatures come apart, exposing the threads that bind them together. People ask me, she says, What is this "Cloud Net"?

With an hour or so gone by she says she admires her colleagues who put a watch on the lectern when they do a reading. She loosens the threads that bind her audience, smiling as she returns their applause.

MAPPING THE ROOT OF RESPONSE

ART IN GENERAL, NEW YORK, NY, MAY 19, 1999

Jena Osman

Site 1: City of Notes, State of Net, Cloud Country

In the middle of the gallery, a giant white net. More of a web really, for a colossal spider preparing to take over the world. The cotton looks pulled and fluffy, as if it were just about to be fed into a loom. Instead, the web is suspended from the ceiling, just low enough that it feels like a big decision to walk beneath it. A viewer (particularly a viewer my size) could walk beneath parts of it, but only carefully. It invites me to take the risk—to put my head in the linear clouds—and if no one else was here, maybe I would.

Nets are connectors, but webs are traps. Webs are connectors, but nets are traps. Weaving is a good metaphor for etymological empowerment (ancient cultures connect at the root of a word and then spin outward), but the art form is also implicated in modern day commercial oppression (sweatshops). I'm not surprised that Vicuña's project presents me with these paradoxical conversations.

The *cloud-net* piece is an extension of Vicuña's interest in the quipu—an ancient writing system where language was actually communicated by a system of woven threads and knots. What is primary in the quipu and in weaving in general, is that threads and knots are woven together and then have the equal potential to be undone or unraveled. In fact, this huge cloud net was woven and then unraveled in three different galleries in three different cities (Buffalo, Houston, New York), each time, interacting with the space quite differently. And this is a good trope for how Vicuña treats words as we know them. On the one hand, she weaves them together to make poems or songs, but on the other hand, she peels away their layers—unravels them down to their originary etymologies. When things start to unravel, they also create momentary connections between meanings (*precarios*—>Latin for precarious—>precis—>prayer; net—>next—>knot; rot—>red). In the chaos of unraveling, a different order of contact is possible.

Site 2: Poet's Table, Precarious State

In a small alcove I find "the poet's table" where a number of small sculptures made of everyday "residual" materials are assembled. In routine circumstances, these scraps and pieces would be considered detritus, except that Vicuña has reinvented them, re-released them as fantastical forms. These are what Vicuña calls "precarios," in that their material existence is ephemeral, entirely dependent on the angle at which we approach them. I write down their names:

quilo	crashed pencils
hilos tembleque	círculo del canosto de la basura
red de plumas	walker st
poncho vacío	fiery brain
lápiz enarbolado	red blanca torcida
grid fuchsia	NY light
fleece ball	hilillos
lápiz de gonzalo	persiana quipu
cuadrado vacío	telar imposible

Vicuña says "clouds are the ethical model of what is to come." I interpret this to mean that clouds are the point where energy gathers from the earth and the atmosphere, but that energy is then released back to the earth and atmosphere in another form. There is a reciprocity, a cycle of recycling. The poet's table is a material/grounded manisfestation of that ethics. Another quote from Vicuña: "There will only be equality where there is reciprocity. The root of the word 'respond' is to offer again, to receive something and offer it back."

Site 3: Video City, Eco-Greco-planet

A short film plays on a tv monitor at the back of the gallery. Dancers hold long cords of thick white thread on a pier. The screen says:

playing a harp of silence
we will all go away
un less
a new net
worth
is born

The three dancers in the film seem to be the three Fates, weaving lifespans in thread. Other Greek weavers: Arachne turned into a spider by Athena. Ariadne giving Theseus a liberating ball of thread. These stories twist alongside the contemporary threads of the World Wide Web, the stock exchange, trade—Vicuña makes the puns visible, dedicating her project to the "future ancient weavers."

During the credits of the film, the following fact is relayed: "during the 6th extinction period 30,000 species are disappearing a year." Something has gone wrong with the cultural translation of the word "respond"—the root is no longer there.

Site 4: Non-intentional Nation of Attentions

The performance begins with Vicuña connecting the audience with string, before sitting under the net to read. At each of her readings, Vicuña listens to what is happening in the room and incorporates the ambient material into the performance. Because of this, there is always an element of surprise, of improvisation. At Art in General, the ambient elements are like an insurgency. Just about everything that could disrupt our focus does so. The sound system isn't working correctly. The elevator door is tremendously noisy—like a garage door opening, accompanied by a game-show bell. The floors themselves are very "responsive"—offering something back for each step they receive. People continue to arrive with the door-bell-creak chorus almost until the very end of the performance. How can Vicuña, with her very quiet reading voice, make her part of the conversation heard?

While waiting for the first elevator-full of latecomers to be seated, she sings a song that is simply "weaving clouds weaving clouds…again and again and again." While singing, she unravels a thread from a ball of yarn and throws it to Felix Bernstein, who is about 8 (?) years old. Felix grabs the thread, Cecilia pulls, and the thread snaps back into her hands. She makes a game of this giving, holding, and snapping-back sequence, repeating it several times. The image of grabbing for the string only to have it pulled away is like an image of my process of attention during the entire reading. Just as I think I can access the words that are being said, they are torn from my ear by an external sound in the room.

Vicuña tells a story about a girl playing in the skies with a clay pot. Her brother comes and breaks the pot, and (do I hear this correctly?) the world is created by the water flowing out around the shards. In writing this, I realize that memory and ambience are two common phenomena, both calling attention to the sensation that there is a wholeness that can only be perceived in fragments. Even with the help of an incredibly obscured videotape, I can only glean small parts of Vicuña's performance. Further shards:

—Vicuña tells the paradox of Plato condemning the poets, saying that poetry can only imitate reality, and yet he must tell this in a poem. In this room where the poems escape into the noisy atmosphere, with only small parts remaining, I think this is not an imitation of reality, but experience itself.

—suddenly a new noise is heard: a loud humming emanating from the walls. Vicuña notes it and tells a story of when the Indians came to Lima looking for a job. When they arrive, they hear a loud humming that they assume is coming from a giant being, when in fact it was simply the sound of cars, faxes, all the machines humming at once. "This humming is eating us up as we try to speak."

—the story of the Eskimo who fell into the frigid water and was able to survive because he remembered the words "it's not cold."

—"each one of us a fragment in the shaft of light."

I gather all of these fragments together now, as I did during the actual performance. They are threads that I weave together, lines that I draw from one remote location to another—not to create a totality, but to map a momentary system of connection.

SEED SPEAKINGS: THE POTENTIAL OF SOME ANCIENT IDEAS CONCERNING SEEDS

KRANNERT ART MUSEUM, UNIVERSITY OF ILLINOIS, URBANA-CHAMPAIGN, SEPTEMBER 21, 1999

Linda Duke

I have witnessed Cecilia Vicuña performing her beautiful, dangerous poetry a handful of times, but the first time was in the Fall of 1999, at Krannert Art Museum at the University of Illinois, Urbana-Champaign. Why do I call her poetry dangerous when it harms no one? Why not instead call the poet courageous or the poetry daring? I call Cecilia's poetry dangerous and its performance transgressive because it speaks a truth that has no validity in contemporary American society. Her performance that September night revealed and opened a wound, mourned a loss, and celebrated a possibility that cannot be acknowledged by us collectively but that I feel is known by each of us, individually, to be true.

The audience was seated that evening, restlessly chattering in a large gallery space that had been cleared to make room for 300 or so folding chairs. The program was titled "Seed Speakings: The Potential of Some Ancient Ideas Concerning Seeds." It was part of the most prestigious annual lecture series at the University of Illinois: The George A. Miller Committee's MillerComm Lectures. MillerComm has a reputation for bringing to campus some of the most well-known and respected scientists, humanists, philosophers, and leaders from all spheres of society. The Museum's curator of contemporary art, Leslie Brothers, and I nominated Cecilia for the series. Our nomination was successful in great part because of the support of the Exhibitions Working Group (EWG), an ad hoc group of faculty, academic professionals and researchers at the University who shared our sense that Cecilia was somehow important to our fin de siècle moment of questioning and experimentation. In Cecilia's art and poetry, and in the trajectory of her life's work—especially "On Behalf of the Seeds"—we saw a model that gave us hope: for art connected with life in a manner both new and ancient, and for healing poetry that might empower us, in turn, to heal with our work. Cecilia represented to us the potential for change.

Leslie made the introduction, a tribute to Cecilia's role as a feminist artist whose dignified steadiness of purpose over a period of 25 years had arguably been more powerful than strident assaults on art world conventions. While Leslie spoke I was distracted. I couldn't help noticing that Cecilia was not preparing for her "lecture" in any of the usual ways. She was by herself, in a shadowy back corner of the room, seeming to focus her energies inwardly. Was she meditating? Feeling a little anxious, I noticed something in her hands: several large dried seed pods in each. Even while Leslie continued to speak, Cecilia began to sway and gently shake the pods. The low rustling sound of this action was mingled with her half-whispered voice—rhythmic, chanting. Leslie completed her introduction and invited everyone to welcome the lecturer. The audience clapped, expecting their speaker to stand up from the front row or enter from the wings. As the clapping awkwardly died down, no speaker took the podium. People waited, uneasily.

Those in the back rows became aware first. Cecilia was slowly moving up the center aisle, but not steadily. Chanting in a louder, almost hissing whisper now, sometimes pausing to shake the pods over a particular person or to gently lay them for a few seconds upon someone's head, she was making her way toward the front of the room. Some people stared straight ahead, perhaps wishing for this strange and unexpected interlude to end; others turned full around in their chairs to watch a process which felt more ceremonial than academic. Swaying, smiling dreamily, Cecilia continued. I was struck by the mindfulness of her movements and, especially, of her touch. It was almost as though she blessed the audience members whose heads received the pods. I could understand only some of her words, partly because of the unfamiliar cadence of her voice, and partly because some of the words did not seem to be English. I could catch bits of Spanish, but she seemed to be casting her net wider than a Spanish-English dichotomy. By the time she reached the microphone, I could sense that her speech had become more narrative. She was delivering a kind of inspired etymology that crossed language boundaries freely. Oddly, the effect was to make even the English terms sound exotic. It was, for me, as though she opened a hole in a wall that had defined the parameters of languages my whole life. What if such a reliable barrier fell away? I was changed by that instant.

I want to mention something odd that seems important. When Cecilia's strange vocalizations were in recognizable English, I felt myself squirming. A "foreign" word could sound beautiful and mysterious when drawn out long and woven into the song-like chant; but when I heard English words and phrases delivered in this manner, it felt embarrassing to the point of taboo. The way the poet chanted in a mixture of languages strangely humbled the English, relieved it of the privileged position my culture accords it. I think now that the effect of hearing my everyday language spoken as poetry—an experience rarely had by most Americans—was one of the most lasting of the evening. I still wince and yet am fascinated. I said that this bastardizing humbled the English, but it did more than that.

Simultaneously Cecilia's delivery revealed a subversive power in English words—words such as "art" or "odor" or "seeds"—that had previously seemed mild-mannered and self-evident. What if the words we use every day carry within them the potential for change? What if ancient knowledge lies buried there, still accessible to us?

On the day before her performance Cecilia had looked with interest at some of the ancient Andean ceramic objects and textiles in the Museum's collection. She requested slides of some of these to show the audience. So the program now became a slide talk, but not in the usual sense. Cecilia wanted the audience to see certain ancient images as she spoke her poetry. I think I understand better now than I did then why this was important. And I think that maybe all of her drawings, her installations, her performative actions over the years have had the same function as those slide images of ancient forms and lines in the Seed Speakings performance. Maybe those simplified, symbolic forms and acts are so useful because they embody very large understandings that cannot be conveyed using ordinary sentences or even a single human language. Just as computers can compress data in order to transmit over the Internet what would be too sprawling and—curiously—too easily corrupted if it were not concentrated and simply packaged, so I believe Cecilia uses visual images in her work to transmit to her audience understandings—most of them ancient beyond measure—that cannot be communicated otherwise. They cannot be "unpacked" collectively, the way an art historian unpacks the significance of an image in a lecture. The ancient images Cecilia shows must be delivered in their unmediated, compressed form, to be opened by each individual audience member. She speaks to us while we view the slides, almost perfoming a midwifery for our hearts as they open in response. Cecilia looks at the images with us, speaking about them in a way that fascinates but also feels inappropriate.

"Dangerous" and "transgressive" are words I used at the beginning of this reminiscence: the uncomfortable laugh, the sense of something icky or frightening, of shame, of curiosity, of disorientation, and yet also of opening, of possibility. Transgression is a particular category of dangerous act. It implies the sense of taboo and it threatens something more than personal safety. I remember once hearing performance artist Joe Goode say that "intuition is always transgressive." He was right, of course. I think now that aesthetic experience itself is transgressive in America. Perhaps the experience of poetry has been transgressive in many cultures; but maybe others have made more generous accommodations for its continued existence, even as they contained its dangerous power.

I can't even remember how the presentation ended. I don't think I was the only one who felt a bit disconcerted. I imagine there were people who left that night feeling annoyed or misled or just plain baffled. Others, I saw, were moved. Seed Speakings took place so many years ago and has stayed, still compressed in my mind, all that while. Asked to write about it here, I am amazed at what stayed with me: the senses of ceremony, of deep ambivalence, and of beauty.

READEME THE BINARY

UNIVERSITY OF MINNESOTA'S RARIG CENTER, APRIL 2001

Maria Damon

Quipu or khipu is an Inca textile signifying system, sister to abaci, hieroglyphs, runes and alef-beitic writings but different in a signal senso-tactilic respect. Comprising, like a contemporary computer language, a series of binaries (knots and twinings either left-to-right or right-to-left, one-threaded or two-threaded, overhand or underhand, etc), each of which has different meaning, it is a system of tied woollen-twine-cordage knots: in other words, textile, true to the western-etymological nexus of text as textile, from texere, or weaving. The arrangement of knots making up the cloth—text? accounting ledger? hanging? "soft sculpture"? "fiber-art"?—is literally meaningful in the same way that arrangements of letters in linear succession are meaningful—"literally"; the knots could be said to be letters as well as numbers, conveying conceptual, informational, poetic and other kinds of knowledge. When in April 2001 Cecilia Vicuña entered the performance space—organized as a theater-in-the-round—at the University of Minnesota's Rarig Center, she encircled that space—and on occasion, random members of us, the audience—with red and white yarn, twisting it under around and through the slats in chairs, our fingers, etc. in order to secure it. We were webbed into ("interpellated" in another, sonic/theoretical as well as visual/textilic idiom) her universe of signification, which included, besides the semen/blood lineage she materialized through white/red sibling skeins, chanting, movement around the room and slides of the threads in other—Andean—contexts projected on a large screen at the far end away from us. This red and this white create the world, she told us in words I don't remember.

More than two years later, August 2003, she sends me the notes for the performance. "Sky-tinted Water." Was that really the piece she performed? There seems no point of overlap in content between what I experienced then in the dark roomful of people breathing and what I read now on the page. But in method there is always lineage, continuity. The concern with etymology woven through and thematized in all the work is quipuesque—words are knots along the thread of history, the thread of language, and ultimately they must all be related in a subtle web of kinship that carries across time, national borders, vast oceanic unknowns, sporic diasporas textualized or sounded. And the spiraled concentricity of concept and execution is consistent across the body of Vicuña's work as well: the roundness of the then-April space, girded by the tensile strength of two strands of yarn, and the now-August writings in circles on the white page, one thought-thread generating the next in a series of whorls, creating lace of letters in artfully random design—the delicacy of both enterprises enables our entry into a precious space—page or stage or, in Aristotle's term, mental image—that is and is not bounded, by breath so tracive it hovers in a liminal zone where phenomena exist and do not (this zone must be the realm of Imagination!)—these arcs of letters and word fragments wending back through Latin Sanskrit Indo-European, not to mention transcontinental homophonic leaps from Inka to Spanish to English (as in the coinage "quiPoem"), take us back to the marriage of thing and thought, breath and idea, world and sound. A creation myth is recreated every day, out of the everyday matter of breath and cloth, eating, sleeping, speaking, breathing.

The Binary as a concept has taken a severe beating in post-'68 literary theory and criticism, as it is tied in to Western civilization's tendency to reify all phenomena, experience, concepts, and objects into good or bad, desirable or undesirable—in other words, binaries are always envisioned as strict, mutually exclusive, and worst of all, arranged in a hierarchy that elevates one term over the other. Vicuña's use of the binary, though, joins others' breakthrough inventions of various processes intended to make duality more of a duet, a generative, (re)productive à la spermwhite-bloodred, not necessarily predictable process, a romantic and elemental courtship of sameness and difference. The dialectic is one such strategy, in which ideas are created when one moves from a stand-off of two opposites into a merged third entity which in turn generates its own opposite, etc.—or the less deterministic and random "dialogic" process, which does not implicitly promise progress but generates activity through dynamic oscillation rather than orderly negotiation. Kamau Brathwaite's coinage, the "tidalectic" process, permits a trope specific to his experience of Caribbean ocean culture's elemental cycles of movementhistory, natureculture, bodymindheart, ebbflow, etc. Vicuña also rehabilitates (reclothes) the bin(d)ary as one that is non-hierarchical and non-fixed, more supple than the dialectic, less random than the dialogic, more rigorous than the tidalectic. Vicuña's intertwined white-and-red yarn, by creating a closed but permeable space, an island of receptivity, opens us participants into a plurifiscent place of generosity generativity.

Cecilia Vicuña, out of the legend (reading) of her generative exile, a political tragedy, created of us a text-isle, littorally, strung with hymns, knots of receptive audio-vibrancy, loose ends tasseled and untied, filiated filaments unflummoxed and tentacles reaching toward each other, streaming outward for the stimulation of each others' communitasse from which to drink hungthirstily in our core elementalities. Intertextuated, we revel in her unraveling, spelling/ binding gossamer sonority, soft-precarious and we strain to hear a keening, to catch with our kenning-challenged hear-hands. A precise marriage of sensory and cerebral, perceptive and affective, knowing and knotting, nodding and no-ing.

UNIVERSITY OF TEXAS OF THE PERMIAN BASIN

ODESSA, APRIL 11, 2002: A TRANSCRIPTION BY KENNETH SHERWOOD

[Melodious Chant - Vocables]

a la salud ustedes
salud

ahhh

ay ay ay ay

gracias a todos por venir
gracias a ken por traer me
gracias a todos

you all understand that don't you?

gracias
you know
what's the origin of the sound GRAA

GRAAAAAAAA

he thinks its very funny doesn't he

graaaaaaaa
gra in its most ancient form
is heart

and the idea is that when you say gra
it's like saying heart aloud
so each time you say gra cias
it's like you bring the Aloudness
of the heart
back

heart aloud
gracias concha y tu mar

graaaa
graaaaaaaaaaciassss

. . . .

it was hard to come in
inside
because outside
you know you have this terrace
you've been to this terrace?

so you can lie flat
watching the falcons

play a game with the swallows

and the swallows do just like the hummingbirds
they pretend
that light
is flashing
on their bodies

TAH they go like that
and turn the ray
in a different direction
so I will begin
with a hummingbird poem for you
because this is what they do
some of these creatures they have
this is the males
they have this red plumage
here in the front of their breast

and this is how they catch the females
they play with the light in such a manner
Tah they go like that
and Fum, throw a ray of light
so she
will catch
the one
that throws the best
rays of light

La luz

es el primer animal visible de lo invisible.

Light

is the first visible animal
of the invisible.

That's
Lezama
Lima

Tienes algo que communicar, Colibrí?
Lanzas rayos
colibrí?
el jugo de tus flores
evidentemente
te ha mareado Colibrí
lanza rayos
lanza rayos,
colibrí
i
that's
Chiripá Guaraní

Have something to say,
Hummingbird?
Hummingbird flashes
rays of light
The juice from your flowers
has made you dizzy
Hummingbird flashes
rays
of light!

Ten

tenelaire
Zun Zun

La luz

Traga néctar
lumbrón

Espejo
que vuela

Oro tornasol

Cáliz
corola
bicho fulgor

Vence a la muerte

Altarci to licór

Light plays upon you

[you] sip
nectar

[nectar in death]
bird-fly
[fly in death]
Mirror in flight

Iridescent gold
Chalice of petals

[shine shine] shining critter

beat death

nectarine

liquor shrine

Child licking Sip sip

Chupá
[chupá chupá] picaflor!

Nadie es lo frágil
Quicker than quick
heart
beats
Pico en perfume
Flying prism
light of the edge

I'm off
to work
Ven a
trabajar

Viso y derrumbe

Cálamo zúm

Humming [the] feather
Dream
whirringdon't
stop!
Gracias

el pobrecito hummingbird I
I had not thought of him

do you have them around here?
[Yes]

They've been hiding from me though

I haven't seen them around
and
I never saw before the association between that
the red light
somehow in you made me think
it was really them
doing it

in reality
when I thought of showing you this film

it's because that film
I did in 1999

years before it all happened

do you remember that line
that says

we will all
go away
unless
a new
net

worth

is born

imagine the worth
of the whole
net
as a new
net
worth

imagine that

imagine too
that this is my second 11th of september

imagine that in the second
for you
it's the second
because for you this one will always be the first

but for me the first
is 1973

do you remember the american pilots flying chilean planes
to bomb la moneda in Santiago
do you remember that

remember that
remember that flight

forgotten in threads
forgotten in threads
forgotten in silence

as if it never ever ever happened

gone into the black black hole

gone
gone

form addresses shadow
T'ao Ch'ien says

form
into the shadow

peace

peace

do you know what's inside the word peace

LOOK at the word
it is not a word at all
it is a state
it is an inner core
it is
something I cannot even see
here in the page
the scribbling goes round
I cannot see
it says the three are a trellis
the first meaning of peace was a trellis
a trellis of hands?
no
a trellis for vines?
no
a trellis of words?
no

the origin of page
a pact
pact in peace
an accord
as if the page agrees
to be

with us
as if we're in accord
waiting waiting for an accord

as if the page
the sound of the page is bound together
with us
as if the sound of this page
is moving
about

is moving about
is moving
about

imagine the sound of writing
bringing about the page

the page of peace
are we in the same page you say?
are we in the same pact
pacting peace
are we of the peace
do you say

do you say a peace
pact pact pact

the word comes to you
as a bird to a nest
who is she
who is she
it comes from others to you

does it come to you
it dwells in you
it speaks in you
it comes in you

walkers on a dry sea
on a deep blue sea

someone asked
what is this permian basin
floating about
floating about this dark oily sea

we are the walkers of the dry sea
the walkers of the dry sea

last night
we were on the fourth floor of this building
looking out into the dry sea
people flying kites
kites against a deep blue sky

floating about
the dark dark oil

going up in flames
going up in flames
going up in flames

CARDINAL FORMANTS: EMPLACEMENT, TANGENCE, WITNESS, RAPT

Kenneth Sherwood

Emplacement

we are the walkers of the dry sea
the walkers of the dry sea

It risks becoming a commonplace to image the post-industrial *estadounidense* as a driver cruising in Humvee, and for whom, even clotted in suburban gridlock, there is no *place*—but roads, networks, multi-lane shunts that bypass by design the particulars of place or locale. Reading Vicuña on the hummingbirds chasing automobile tail-lights that pierce the smog of Santiago streets, one suspects that she knows El Autopista del Sur of Cortazar, in which an unreal cessation in traffic flow brings travelers out of their automotive shells to enter a mutual space, a flickering of utopia before the movement is resumed. Premonition of the local, lost.

Vicuña speaks "on location," in situ, eschewing compass and G.P.S. As one learns from Dennis Tedlock, this is not anomalous but fundamental to such "other Americans" as the Zuni or the Maya. And not just at the scale of architecture or monument or ritual act, but as a function of everyday living. Vicuña orients herself—to the cardinal points (or four directions), the wind, light, topography and ecology—with equal intensity whether gazing from high in a university building in upstate New York or scanning the horizon in west Texas.
Accessed again with texts, audio tapes, and notes sitting beside one, the performances overlay physical spaces and remembered locales: the canvas "Ode to Joy" hangs behind the podium in Capen Hall, Buffalo, New York . . . a flotilla of ice shards sweeps towards the falls at Niagara . . . late light tinctures the tributaries of the St. Johns River become earth's veins in Jacksonville, Florida . . . wisp of Swallows sweeps above the flatness of the Permian Basin in Odessa, Texas. Each performance begins in place, bringing it—the placeness of

the place—freshly to the minds of the locals who should (but as often do not) know it. Then the coming inside, entrance into a performance space and the space of language.

it was hard to come in
inside
because outside
you know you have this terrace
you've been to this terrace?

Plural Tangence

do you know what's inside the word peace
look at the word
it is not a word at all

Or it is not a word in the fixed, singular sense. The event creates a pluralized space, employing various media. But more than the simple multiplication of media—a chanted song, the silent video of dancing figures weaving, the images of a cloud-net, rays of light (threads) superimposed upon poet, audience, screen, room—it is an effect of tangence.

The book. Joining in space and through sight/sound from tangent to tangible (from *tangere*, to touch). In: touching the linguistic dimension. On: touching the visual dimension. Off: touching the temporal dimension. Words' forms weighed and weighted, assuming sound shapes, page shapes. Before us, language transpiring (breathing), "connecting" through patterns of repetition, etymological riffs, puns, and rhymes.

imagine the sound of writing
bringing about the page

the page of peace
are we in the same page
you say?
are we in the same pact
pacting peace

The performativity brought to her readings foregrounds less the expressive spontaneity associated with improvisation, and more a kind of listening. Roland Barthes writes: "...whereas for centuries listening could be defined as an intentional act of audition (to listen is to want to hear, in all conscience), today it is granted the power of playing over unknown spaces...listening grants access to all forms of polysemy, of overdetermination, of superimposition...by definition, listening was applied; today we ask listening to release...."[102] Place the performance/transcription of "Tentenelaire Zun Zun" (Zit Zit, Hummingbird) against the pages of *Unravelling Words & The Weaving of Water.*[103] Grounded in the text, a virtuoso crossing between languages unfolds. The conventional bi-lingual page of the translation enforces a kind of cultural separatism; in the performance, a fusion or melding creates a new, local arrangement—in Spanish and English, with lines omitted, repeated, reordered—a new versioning.

Versioning—creating new arrangements of a poem during performance—shifts our orientation towards *the* poem, or the *Vicuña* poem. Nick Piombino writes: "There is a distinction that can be made between written works that can be appreciated by means of ordinary silent reading and those in which each word should be heard read aloud or individually sounded out aloud in the mind. With the latter works readers are encouraged to experience the poem by sounding it out internally in a process of concentrated, yet freely imaginative listening and reading."[104]

---

102. "Listening," in *The Responsibility of Forms: Critical Essays on Music, Art, and Representation.* Trans. Richard Howard. U California, 1991. 58.
103. Vicuña, 74-79.
104. Nick Piombino. "The Aural Ellipsis and the Nature of Listening in Contemporary Poetry." *Close Listening: Poetry and the Performed Word.* Ed. Charles Bernstein. New York: Oxford University Press, 1998. 62.

The witnessing of a performance encourages one to begin to read as a listener, entering and stretching the language itself and the "texts" of the poems. We sound out the words in an echo of the composing process. Vicuña embodies the "poet [as] researcher who must listen closely to the sounds and voices of actuality to discover where the poetry may exist within it."[105]

are we of the peace
do you say

do you say a peace
pact pact pact

Burnt Witness

the word comes to you
as a bird to a nest
who is she
who is she
it comes from others to you

does it come to you
it dwells in you
it speaks in you
it comes in you

Here oral performance exploits the mutable, the fusion of syllables and tongue. The page, the sounding. Sounding takes the form of a resistance to forgetting, *as if it never ever ever happened*. Sounding and forging, as if every ever happened.

Somehow the performances foreground the ethical, historical, and political in their enframing of a communitarian space. Whispered, gestured towards: the

105. Ibid. 65.

towers and the architecture. Here too resonates Nathaniel Mackey's observation on the experiencing of September 11th not as a sudden crisis but as part of an ongoing catastrophe. For Vicuña, there is the need to construct poems amid some thirty or more years of dust and debris.

Ears hear: The word comes to you /as a burnt witness.

Chatter After Rapt

Doors opened to a performance and the space was filled, or rather syllables performed its dimensions. Words as worlds as warders, watchers offering themselves up, leaving the memory of shared space and words. Then from the audio file which runs on past the end: sightless digitized sound replicates a space, a vertiginous, stereo simulation. Shifts, tensions, patterns as invisible migrations across a transparent sky, or the settling into order of tracks across a blank field. Voices cluster, breaking the crust and the words rush back as air into a vacuum. High-fidelity chatter after rapt.

THE POETRY PROJECT AT ST. MARK'S CHURCH
NEW YORK, NY, MAY 15, 2002

Cecilia Vicuña

Vicuña writes to her mother regarding the St. Mark's performance on May 15, 2002:

yes, mami, it was the most beautiful reading in the world for me. as always, i begin not knowing what i am going to do. i am introduced, people applaud, and as they wait, i don't make a move. i am nowhere to be found. i sit quietly, in the back, with a spool of white thread in my hand, and suddenly, i lift the spool and make it spin, as if it were a spindle. and at that moment i realize that i, too, have become a living spindle and begin to listen to its slight sound, almost imperceptible. while turning, and without thinking, I begin to do a little dance beneath the spindle, placing the spindle next to the ears of some people, so that they too can hear it turning. i walk down the wide aisle in the center of the hall. mimicking my movements, the thread begins to fall to the floor, like a small cascade, undulating back and forth: it goes forward as I approach the stage, then back again, until it forms a tangle. then I take the spool and throw it forward, towards the podium. once there, i grab the end of the thread and put it in my mouth, saying: "That is my mother" and I begin to sing a little song, as if in your voice, and say: "that is what she would do, with a thread in her mouth," and I continue to sing and read the poem from my new book that is dedicated to you. when i am done, everyone is like in another world, and it is difficult to return to this one. it is a gesture of love towards you, who taught me to weave and play with thread while singing, as you do. ¿le gustó?

love, your cec

[Translated from the Spanish]

"LINK, LINK, LINK PLEASE"

THE POETRY PROJECT AT ST. MARK'S, NEW YORK, NY, MAY 15, 2002

Juliana Spahr

In graduate school, we spent a lot of time in seminars arguing about that Auden line "poetry makes nothing happen." The truth or untruth of this line was something we debated as if our lives depended on it. And to some extent, our lives did. The truth or untruth of this line would impact our writing and how we saw others' writing, would privilege a different set of works, would require us to direct our attention in various directions. It would force us to consider weighty issues—like who we wrote with and on, and why and how that choice perhaps wasn't only about what interested us. Once we realized literature as a crucial part of any political movement, then we would also end up with a different canon and different issues to discuss and with different sorts of activism in our lives.

I think many people left those seminars agreeing with Auden. And probably just as many left disagreeing. I just left them confused. I could tell a personal story about how poetry mattered to me, how it had dramatically changed my thinking about things, and how it had reshaped my brain in ways that I couldn't have done on my own or even with the help of various psychoactive drugs. It was clear to me that poetry changed my life very profoundly socially (the poets that I counted as friends) and intellectually (how, say Ginsberg's *Howl* blew my mind in high school, starting off a whole chain of events where I realized I didn't have to follow my peers down the path of right-wing bigotry and narrow-mindedness because my thinking that wasn't the way to go now had a whole literature behind it). I was changed. My mind was changed.

I think sometimes that the reason we had to have this endless debate about the Auden line (and it was just that, a debate about a line: we didn't really debate the context of the Auden line or the larger resonances of the poem; we weren't, to tell the truth, even all that interested in Auden) was that we were thinking of audience, not thinking of alliance. We weren't sure there was an audience outside of ourselves for this work. We really couldn't even talk to fellow graduate students outside of our seminar about these issues in contemporary writing because most of them didn't even read it or see it as having any influence. One of the guiding assumptions of much of graduate school was that contemporary literature didn't matter and if it did, it was only good for uplift of marginalized communities within the United States (the sort of argument that goes: it might matter for these poor people over there but I'm so beyond that).

Cecilia Vicuña came to read in the middle of one of these discussions.[106] And her reading was a "crrrakkk" for me, the sort of "crrrakk" that she locates in *Antologia de la poesia surrealista*.[107] Her reading changed my thinking. Through her work I stopped seeing "experimentation" as something that white, middle-class Americans were partial towards and started seeing the things that get called experimental in the United States as part of a long and large tradition that is much wider than the West. Her reading was all about alliance. In this reading, Cecilia began with myth and breathing, then India and the Spanish language, then the Indo-European languages and Lima and Santiago. In this reading it is clear that her work is all about alliance, about threads, about connections, about responsibilities to the histories of words and languages, and how they shape us.

Cecilia's work relentlessly points out that saying literature doesn't matter does not let one off from having to think about how *it might matter*. I remember once, this is years later, talking with her about how the Hawai`i tourist authorities had brought over some French artists and their art. Among the art was a giant cage filled with parakeets. Many people did not go to the presentations by the French artists because they felt that things French had to be boycotted as long as the French continue to test their nuclear bombs in the Pacific. But some people went because they wanted to ask the French artists what their work had to say about how the French continued to test nuclear bombs in the Pacific. When asked, the French artists didn't really have a reply. I remember telling Cecilia this story because I was confused about it. I couldn't decide if it was a little mean to expect the French artists to necessarily have a

106.Spahr refers to a performance at SUNY Buffalo on March 10, 1994; a transcription by Kenneth Sherwood is available on the University at Buffalo's Electronic Poetry Center: <http://www.wings.buffalo.edu/epc/rift/rift04/vicu0401.html>

107. See Vicuña's performance-lecture at the Feminisms & the Avant-Garde Conference above.

position in their work on nuclear testing in the Pacific. And I remember her stating that the question was a legitimate one and that even if an artist just puts a bunch of parakeets in a cage, he still has to deal with questions of nuclear testing. Again, the "crrrakkk."

When I look at Cecilia's work, especially the performance pieces that are collected in "Ten Metaphors in Space,"[108] I see her putting the parakeets in the cage for a reason. In one, Cecilia spills a glass of milk on the sidewalk in response to the 1,920 children who died that year from drinking milk that was contaminated by distributors. Or she fills a gallery with leaves in dedication to socialism.

This attention to the questions is what I find so powerful in her work. Not just the alliance question but how the alliance question filters into the languages question—not only how the colonial languages of Spanish and English intersect with their differing power relationships but also how Spanish intersects with Mapuche or Quechua or Nahuatl. In a reading that she did at the Poetry Project in May of 2002 all of these issues come to the forefront. She opens with a song that she attributes to her mother, a mother who she says always puts the thread in her mouth. The song moves to English back to Spanish and at moments into some space between languages. As I listened to this recording the other day, I swear that at one point she sings the word "grammatical" and at another moment "the drone of speech." But I'm not sure. This song, this piece, ends with her moving between the words "ecstasy" and "estar." If there is anything that this performance is about it is those big words like connection, alliance, and affiliation. The connections are clearly established between languages, the threads that we hold in our mouths, in the back-and-forth that she does as she performs. But that serves as only a metonym for a whole series of other connections. Later in the performance she tells the story of watching Muhammad Ali in Santiago: "when he said I am pretty, we felt we were pretty; when he said I am black, we thought we were black. It was a shock to come to the United States and realize we were not black after all." From there she moves to the back-and-forth of the financial debt, to demonstrations against nuclear weapons, to the United States's and Chile's September 11th, then back to the debt. In the middle of all this she mentions "word associations, rapid shifts of

108. See Vicuña's *Unravelling Words and the Weaving of Water.* 12-23.

attention, ungrammatical strings" and then pleads "link, link, link please; link my struggles; no, it says my string."

In an interview with David Levi Strauss,[109] Cecilia says "I am a mixed person, a person of two cultures. So I don't trust either—that is the reality. I use everything because I want to ask them all to remember. I write, I sing, I weave at the same time, because I'm at the moment of emergency, at the moment of danger, when you actually feel that all of this could go away." I find it striking that in her work she weaves things together but does not merge them into a hybrid whole. "Turn inside-out the you" she commanded us at the Poetry Project in May. In pursuit of this her work connects things with string, connects the two sides of a stream or a street, provisionally, momentarily and then everything looks different for a brief moment.

TERRILOQUIS VICTUS DICTIS :: SPECIES PATEFACTAST VERBIS

PIEROGI ART GALLERY, BROOKLYN, NY, SEPTEMBER 12, 2002

Rodrigo Toscano

"...overborne by terrific utterances :: the face of the words made manifest..."

The date I don't really remember, but not long after 9-11 (2001). A gallery somewhere in Northern Brooklyn. Laura (Elrick) is with me, Mónica de la Torre is there, as is Bruce Andrews, Odile Cisneros, Alan Gilbert, Kristin Prevallet, and others. Poets, essayists, translators, artists, "interested parties."

109· "The Memory of the Fingers: A Conversation between Cecilia Vicuña and David Levi Strauss." *cloud-net*. 18-21.

Bright floodlights (to be dimmed later), the customary red wines flowing, crackers crackling between gleaming teeth. And if memory "serves me"—"correctly," on the walls were sculptures made of rusty wire, squiggly figurative forms I can't make out now.

The typical schmoozy inattention to any one thing and everything all around.

A couple of cultural-scene "lurkers," a handful of just-happened-to-pop-ins from the curbside.

Proprietors, I imagine, one or two might have been present.

The dinkiest utility toilet, typical of galleries like this; you step into it, attempt to gather yourself...*if only for a moment.*

•

Bodies that make up our solidity as a singular organ, but as lone whales suddenly by twos and threes we assemble into chairs.
Thirty or forty of them.

Paradox:

Before the assembly—is assembledness.
Before the assembly—is disassembledness.

mantén esa contradicción entre tus dientes,
y si la sueltas, te diremos, "mejor...para ti"
y si la muerdes como perro rabioso
—nos da igual...en decir..."mejor...para ti"

•

To say,

"I remember (it)" or
"I don't remember (it)"

—both equally romantic—

Is there a better way to describe "it" and its remembrance?

That is, outside of the *pitiable* postmodern present-continuous (capitalist) space?

•

The skin is relentless in its contiguity, as much as a rock face of a mountain, even in its dissolution.

There's no such thing as a "hole" in it (the skin).

For where there might be a singular "hole"—there's still the very non-edges of skin, contiguous until a final dissipation.

Faces.
Familiar or unfamiliar.
Familiarly composed.

Thirty or forty of them.

•

It must have been Regis, or his young protegé whose name I can't recall, or maybe Raoul Sentenat who read before Cecilia. "Must have" because people were applauding...that light after-a-reading (appreciative) patter.

And as it progressed toward its dying-down—assembled there, taut skin of the evening, moist, pored & breathing, *enter* Cecilia—

of the audience as an audience, rises...as the applause dies down, one lone clap continues—hers...at a certain tempo, not of the fastest present there (of those perhaps more agitated than the rest) nor at the tempo of the slowest (of the fatigued perhaps, those feeling a sense of perfunctoriness toward the event, or maybe as an overt expression of the furiously-agnostic cultural critic).

Cecilia's clap, then, begun at the same time as everyone else's, grows slightly louder as the applause dwindles...narrows into the mid-tempo of the audience itself....louder and louder, more pronounced it becomes...

pk' pk' pk' pk'

and steadies there (in volume and pulse)...

pk' pk' pk' pk'

"just *what* is this woman doing?" (no doubt, several are thinking...me too)

and just when the discomfort begins to turn into a strange kind of comfort <tempo>

—*s i l e n c e*—

she stands up and walks toward the podium...never actually arriving there, come to think of it...and perambulates among the audience...

then suddenly, from her lips, a single word, whispered...

we strain to hear it, though the strain seems effortless...

"concha" <silence again>

then a soft flurry of the same word, like leaf stems losing their grip to a sudden gust…

"cooooncha cooooncha cooooncha"

In the English Tongue, conjuring, first of all, a conch shell.
In the Spanish Tongue, that same conjuring, though with the added Chilean demotic tone, denoting "pussy"…also a way of saying "damn."

"cooooncha cooooncha cooooncha"

strangely intimate in our ears, the word swirls and settles there…

(the human ear, it's been noted, is curiously shaped like a conch shell)

did I forget to mention that everyone quivers inside during war-time?

ceaseless
insides
quivering
we were
are

[Fall, 2003]

"Con cha
 cunt má

Madre del tiempo…"

•

The wine, the hubbub, the cultural trappings, the fleeting ambitions, are, for now, distant from our thoughts…now's an all-for-listening…an inside-as-outside / outside-as-inside

assembles us.

A Bruce and a Regis, a Kristin and an Odile, a Cecilia and a me…our social differences, in this not-now now, feel eerily

leveled

"concha!"

•

Who is it?
What is it?

We move in the world…hard-shelled to so much [NYC, USA], borne of so much commonality, and somnambulistically trap it out?

That people gathered here reach toward "it"

commonality? leveling?

•

A question I don't seem to be able to answer,

Is / was the "reading" assembled *before* the event? Or *after* the event?
(me, Mr. Railer, against so many a meta- and pata- physic)

I remember thinking, there, at the reading

"how did we *avoid* this before?"

And the others? In the same not-now now, were they thinking similarly?

•

quivering "what's gonna' happen to me?"

quivering inside, it slowly dwindles

is this fear or serenity?

or both at once?

...

Cecilia then whispers something...but this time a little louder than before:

"they say there's going to be a...

wawawawawa

war"

barely audible, yet the trunk slams down kicking up a cloud of...

And as to whether that was the exact phrase or not, I don't really remember—not long after 9-11 (2001), but the import of it I do...from that not-now now to this.

After the ceaseless ruminating on "it"—the impending strife, horrid conjurer ceaseless, whether as protestors "we," or as lovers late at night snuggling remorse over the state of things…

quivering's

at a standstill

if only for a moment.

As if for the first time…hearing it "they"
"say"
"there-is-going-to-be"
"a"

how did we not *hear* this before?

"concha"

•

Whatever it is, it makes non-poets feel suddenly poetically able-to.

Whatever it is, it makes poets supremely post-'poetically' able-to.

Whatever *name* befits Cecilia's poetry

I don't know, or rather don't remember…

But somehow I *remember* something that's (if only slightly) *ahead* of me…
"but that's impossible!" I say…
(me, Mr. Railer, against so many a meta- and pata- physic)

assembled / disassembled

AT PLAY IN THE PSYCHE OF CYCLES:
CECILIA VICUÑA'S ENDLESSNESSES

Edwin Torres

The universe is my dress
—Kazuo Ohno

The process of occupying one's space is rooted in clarity; a search for, an understanding of, a desire for its lastingness as a way of understanding one's place, one's stance, the posture of our geography within a personal humanity—if each of us is a globe where does territory stop and population begin? It is that shared desire for *understanding*'s elements which illuminates the work of Cecilia Vicuña. The physicality of language as a tool for change embedded within each of us.

Among many locations, I've seen her perform in an art gallery, read at a poetry bar, lecture in an auditorium; and the continuous line at her every appearance is how the audience is presented with a space of their own by bringing hers to the forefront. Whispering into the microphone *inside* her signature whisper, she asks us if we can hear her. Adjusting the relationship to her space between mouth and microphone, between human and machine, so the relationship itself is adjusted not the volume. Our ears are caught, having always been thrown—in a listening that happens with the skin, with the senses.

The audience is the performer's ocean, the ebb and flow of the performance guided by the degree of the audience's involvement. Cecilia presents us with the possibility of helping her shape the message by empowering us—with listening. An audience given a chance to listen is suddenly made aware of its place—an empowering political act, to own your space.

Cecilia's work embodies the role of the griot—the political tied into the personal—as reflected by the territory of sound at her beckon. A word polyglotted into neologistic tendencies will reveal its root, Cecilia grasps this opportunity to delve into the roots and expose hidden wonders, redefinitions, meanings, and new words like seeds waiting to break the dictionary's surface.

The organic entity of the griot manifested as shaman inventing an ecology of language which grows over a lifetime.

What inspires and motivates is how she manages to maintain her singular plurality while traveling from medium to medium. From her book *Instan*, which threads through its pages as a lifeline, a horizon for the viewer to consider, to a benefit for AIDS in Africa where she chanted and slowly dissected the word "aid" while surrounding each layer with its Spanish translation "sida" (which also means care), bringing revery and worship into simultaneous conclusion, transforming the vibrations of the room in three minutes.

Each performance, each reading, each installation, each book has a timeless lineage with no beginning or end. Every time I see her I feel as if she hasn't begun or ended but continued—the storyteller continuing the parable—which lets me bring my history of that moment into the performance. In that liberation, in that mutual exchange is where something new is allowed to happen, for performer and audience.

I thought I'd write about a specific performance of hers performed for only two people, a recording engineer and myself, in the engineer's home-studio, his closet.

The magazine *Rattapallax*, which I co-edited, included an audio CD in every issue. Issue no. 9 featured contemporary Brazilian and American poetry. Cecilia was included on the CD—her voice, a neccesary ground, expanding the reaches of South into North America, plus the chance to record her was too tempting to pass up. We selected a section from her long poem "Se Mi Ya (Seed Me Now See You Later)," which had just been beautifully translated by Rosa Alcalá, and then arranged a recording date to fit into her schedule. We would have an hour of her time to record a three-minute piece.

Late-autumn, New York City on a Saturday morning, orange sun, blue sky, long shadows, winter's around the corner. She arrives at the recording studio, a one-bedroom apartment in lower Manhattan, bundled up for a cold wind yet to blow. In the bedroom is where the computers are—speakers, amps, and a perfectly designed collection of bare-bones hardware needed to drive the ever-growing technology. In the closet is where vocals are recorded, a first-rate microphone and music-stand with clip-on light share the space with neatly hung clothes, shoes on the floor, and tightly rolled socks. It's here that *the magic* happens, creativity captured to live between the ears. The quality is professional, the prices are not! (Sounds like an ad.)

Cecilia has her cache of instruments: seeds, pebbles, bowls, shakers—I had asked her to bring what she needed for a journey into sound. The recording will be her voice on one track, her music on another. I want to use the studio to try to catch what happens in performance by bringing her many facets together within the scope of this brief recording, by using what energy is caught at the moment of its creation and reflecting our surroundings by being implicit *within* them. By layering voice with voice or music we can embody the crux of the text while giving the listener choices on every new listen.

Sitting on the sofa in the living room, we decide to record the music here in the open and proceed to set up the microphone in this environment. It isn't soundproof like the closet, but the energy with the sun streaming in feels right and any minimal outside noise will bring some air and room into the music.

This will be an improvisation of water, seeds, beads, leaves, string and assorted percussives that she's brought with her. We don't know where it'll fit with the words yet, leaving that to chance. We choose not to give her headphones so she can create the music freely without hearing every little tweak. Music like this is created for the microphone, being imperceptible otherwise, as details of breath and listening transfer to music and sound—appropriate for this poem, this poet—to record the macro world under the surface of hearing.

SHE'S SO FINE: CECILIA VICUÑA'S INSTAN

Nada Gordon

(((((magenta light on a dark ground... singing... yellow... neck pulsing... red lasers... it's the breath effort of Cecilia singing... the magenta and yellow shapes move... around & around her wrinkled mouth... back chanting... dry elixir.... word loom star... it's a SPELL ... estrella interior.... the red lasers stripe across the ceiling.... then glow the red yarn... into magic... she hands it to audience members... they touch it.... playing with the light shapes... blank hiss of end of tape sound... someone... Cecilia? ... laughs in the silence... something drops... lights on... I see the yarn is already red and fuzzy... "joyuyuyuyuyuyuyu"... sweet chant & raspy witch voice... beep of cellphones turning off... while she's intoning... song will always supercede poetry... in the thrill of the risk of the performance moment... frail and weird... witchy, pentatonic, wind in bamboo for a minute... sounds like a kid singing to herself on the train... trill... her dimples in the halflight... "gracias"...))))) [Notes Taken at a Performance of Instan, 9/12/2003, New York University][110]

Cecilia Vicuña's work is a meditation on and an enactment of *the fine.*

Not fine as in the sense of "precious" or "luxurious," as in *fine wines* or "she lived surrounded by *finery,*" but fine as in "precise" and "delicate."

Not "delicate" as in weak. Vicuña's *fine* is penetrating and effective, like a string cutting cheese, like laser surgery, like the fine link of the copula in an uncannily exact metaphor.

Not *fine* as in "refined"—which calls up sugar, oil, and pretentious manners. Vicuña's *fine* is the fine of nature, like that of spiders' webs. Or the fine of manipulated nature, like goats mixed genetically with spiders to give silk in their milk. The *fine* of DNA.

---

110. In her introductory note, Gordon refers to a performance in which Vicuña uses slides of the poem-drawings in her book *Instan.*

It is the fine of *lines*. Her book *Instan* is a perfect illustration of the principles of the fine. Simultaneously writing and drawing, as in the Japanese verb *kaku* or the Quechua verb *kellcani*, the pages of the first section of the book, *gramma kellcani (the drawings)*, are reproduced from finely pencilled originals. The printing is in grays, not black, showing the tiny variations of shade characteristic of pencil. Because these variations are the traces of an individual's force and pressure, they serve to humanize the writing and reconnect it with the body of its creator.

The letters in *gramma* ["grandmother" and "grammar" as well as *amma*, "mother"] *kellcani* morph into lines and then back into other letters. Words fuse into lines and then into other words. Sometimes the lines separate to indicate connection but do not actually touch. Sometimes the words arrange in spirals, or crisscrosses, or wave patterns. Some look very like scientific diagrams. Sometimes the words are in Spanish and sometimes they are in English. The drawn lines show how the words are connected and also how they are distinct: *compacto, compose, compartir. Gramma kellcani*, like so many of Vicuña's others, is as much an essay on comparative linguistics and metaphysics as it is a poem as it is a drawing. It is as if Vicuña, unlike Mr. Casaubon in *Middlemarch,* who never manages to find "the key to all mythologies," has truly found, if not the key to all languages, a graphic and probing way into some specific truths about them.

Into the mine of the f(emin)ine.
Or the filaments of the *infinite.*
Or onto the tightrope of the written word into sound and its unpredictable trapeze into meaning.

Ironically, lines as she uses them foil linearity, making the eyeballs dance and loop-de-loop, making the reader turn the book to all angles, maybe even rotate it entirely. What a truly fine way to cause a revolution, to turn the world upside down!

Part Two of *Instan, el poema cognado/the poem*, illuminates the mechanism of the *gramma kellcani* drawings:

An instant is present
it "stands,"
a filament of *sta*, a state of being *stamen*,
a thread in a warp,
a web in ecstasy.

An instant—the smallest divisible unit of time we can experience? At the end of *gramma kellcani* the lines have dispersed into points which are surely stars? They have no more meaning? Except that—wow—they inhabit—nay, they create—the Milky Way, the *fine trickle* of light which is also milk:

To carry back is to relate
a flowing of milk: time
becomes language and love.

And Vicuña's love (in a kind of lightwordmilk), with its dimensions at once personal, political, and metaphysical, transmits as if through a miraculous verbal breast fashioned of the finest fiberoptic technology; "adónde," she asks coyly, as if she truly didn't know she were giving it,

la leche
de una teta
común?

or

a suckling
of musical
ink?

Just as Vicuña's *fine* can be graphic or liquid or light, so also can it be sound, as when in her performances she enters a room first with her voice—*amar / el formans .... formans: "a bunch of frequencies in the human voice" Carlos Guedes*—small (fine) but, even unamplified, capable of filling the huge hall at St. Mark's

Church with its shivery resonances.

A moment of trance where transformation begins:
silence to sound, and back.

NOTES ON THE TEXT

WORKS CITED (INTRODUCTION)

Douglas, Mary. *Purity and Danger: An Analysis of Concepts of Pollution and Danger.* 1966. London: Routledge, 2002.

Fusco, Coco, Ed. *Corpus Delecti: Performance Art of the Americas.* London: Routledge, 2000.

Goffman, Erving. *Frame Analysis: An Essay on the Organization of Experience.* Boston: Northeastern UP, 1974.

Isbell, Billie Jean and Regina Harrison. "Metaphor Spun: A Conversation with Cecilia Vicuña." Vicuña, *The Precarious* 47-57.

Lippard, Lucy. "Spinning the Common Thread." Vicuña, *The Precarious* 7-15.

Martin, Lois. "Immaterial Material & Resonant Thread." *Art Nexus 29* (August-October 1998): 68-72.

McHugh, Heather: An excerpt from "Moving Means, Meaning Moves." *Lofty Dogmas: Poets on Poetics.* Eds. Deborah Brown, Annie Finch, and Maxine Kumin. Fayetteville: U of Arkansas Press, 2005. 277-278.

Méndez-Rámirez, Hugo. "Cryptic Weaving." Vicuña, *The Precarious* 59-71.

Mignolo, Walter D. *Local Histories / Global Designs: Coloniality, Subaltern Knowledge, and Border Thinking.* Princeton, NJ: Princeton University Press, 2000.

Richard, Nelly. "Margins and Institutions: Performances of the Chilean Avanzada." Fusco 203-217.

Rohter, Larry. "So Much Gold, but Andean Farmers See Big Risks, Too." 30 July 2006. *New York Times*. 10 June 2008. < http://www.nytimes.com/>.

Rothenberg, Jerome. "Total Translation: An Experiment in the Presentation of American Indian Poetry." *Pre-Faces & Other Writings.* New York: New Directions, 1981. 76-92.

Sengupta, Somini. "U.S. Sojourn Ends in Debt, and Death by Burial." 13 July 1998. *New York Times.* 10 June 2008. <http://www.nytimes.com/>.

Sherwood, Kenneth. "Sound Written and Sound Breathing." Vicuña, *The Precarious* 73-93.

Spicer, Jack. *My Vocabulary Did This to Me: The Collected Poems of Jack Spicer,* Eds. Peter Gizzi and Kevin Killian. Middletown, CT: Wesleyan UP, 2008.

——. *The House That Jack Built: The Collected Lectures of Jack Spicer.* Ed. Peter Gizzi. Middletown, CT: Wesleyan UP, 1998.

Tedlock, Dennis. *The Spoken Word and the Work of Interpretation.* Philadelphia: U of Pennsylvania P, 1983.

Vicuña, Cecilia. *cloud-net.* Trans. Rosa Alcalá. New York: Art in General, 1999.

——. *perf. and dir. cloud-net.* Bilingual video. Ed. Chris Borkowski. New York, 1998.

——. E-mail to author. 10 February 2003.

———. "Emma Kunz," Trans. Rosa Alcalá. *3x Abstraction: New Methods of Drawing: Hilma af Klint, Emma Kunz, and Agnes Martin.* Eds. Catherine de Zegher and Hendel Teicher. Yale UP, 2005. 121-125.

———. *Instan.* Berkeley, CA: Kelsey St. Press, 2002.

———. "Lecture on the Arts in Chile after 1970." Center for Contemporary Arts, London, 1973.

———. LINEbreak Radio Program. Interview with Charles Bernstein and Performance. September 1995. 15 July 2008. <http://wings.buffalo.edu/epc/linebreak/programs/vicuna/>

———. "Luis Gómez." *XCP: Cross Cultural Poetics.* "Authenticating (Dis)Location/(Dis)Locating. Authenticity" (2001): 52.

———. *Palabra e hilo/Word & Thread.* Trans. Rosa Alcalá. Edinburgh: Morning Star Publications, 1996.

———. Personal interview. 18 July 2001.

———. *Precario/Precarious* (Trans. Anne Twitty). New York: Tanam Press, 1983. N. pag.

———. *The Precarious: The Art and Poetry of Cecilia Vicuña/ Quipoem.* Ed. M. Catherine de Zegher. Trans. Esther Allen. Hanover: University Press of New England, 1997.

———. *Saborami.* England-Latin America: Beau Geste Press, 1973. N. pag.

———. *El Templo.* Trans. Rosa Alcalá. Illus. Manel Lledós. New York: Situations Press, 2001.

———. "Ubixic del Decir, 'Its Being Said.': A Reading of a Reading of the Popol Vuh." Trans. Rosa Alcalá. *"With Their Hands and Their Eyes": Maya Textiles, Mirrors of a World View.* Eds. Mireille Holsbeke and Julia Montoya. Belgium: Etnografisch Museum Antwerpen, 2003. 128-137.

———. *Unravelling Words & the Weaving of Water.* Trans. Eliot Weinberger and Suzanne Jill Levine. Saint Paul, MN: Graywolf Press, 1992.

de Zegher, M. Catherine. "Ouvrage: Knot a Not, Notes as Knots." *The Precarious.* 17-45.

ENDNOTES (INTRODUCTION)

1. See Rodrigo Toscano's essay included in this book.

2. See especially M. Catherine de Zegher's "Ouvrage: Knot a Not, Notes as Knots."

3. An exception is Kenneth Sherwood. Read his essay, "Sound Written and Sound Breathing," as well as his essay included in this book.

4. Additionally, Vicuña has created performances specifically to be filmed; however, the visual effects, editing, and various devices used in making these films, such as the layering of her singing voice over images of an installation, create a much more polished and less interactive experience than do her oral performances in front of a live audience.

5. Marked-up copies of published poems among her performance notes suggest, too, that these are sometimes altered prior to the events.

6. See Sherwood's essay included in this book.

7. Spicer refers to this concept of the poet as a radio in several lectures, which are gathered in *The House That Jack Built*, Ed. Peter Gizzi (see pp. 2, 15, 16-17, 77 and 129). It is also mentioned, along with "counterpunching radio," in the poem "Sporting Life" (see *My Vocabulary Did This to Me: The Collected Poems of Jack Spicer,* Eds. Peter Gizzi and Kevin Killian).

8. See the transcription of Vicuña's 1998 performance at Hallwalls. This, and all other performances cited in this introduction, are transcribed in this book.

9. See Jena Osman's essay included in this book.

10. LINEbreak with Charles Bernstein, 1998 Hallwalls performance, et al.

11. Vicuña's traveling in situ installation, *cloud-net*, included a video, also titled *cloud-net*, of a performance involving three women dancing with and manipulating threads along a Hudson River pier.

12. See Maria Damon's essay included in this book.

13. See Edwin Torres's and Dennis Tedlock's essays included in this book.

14. Goffman, explaining "episoding conventions," writes: "Activity framed in a particular way—especially collectively organized social activity—is often marked off from the ongoing flow of surrounding events by a special set of boundary markers or brackets of a conventionalized kind. These occur before or after the activity in time and may be circumscriptive in space; in brief, there are temporal and spatial brackets" (251). In other words, he clarifies, a gavel would initiate and clearly demarcate court proceedings. Goffman would, I think, also recognize Vicuña's unusual entrance and use of thread at the start of an oral performance as an episoding convention. Interestingly, however, this initiation also marks it as different from the "organized social activity" for which much of the audience has prepared themselves.

In discussing episoding conventions within the oral performance itself, however, I am pointing to the ways in which a poetry reading contains several episoding conventions within it that differentiate preamble from poem, poem from anecdote, poem from poem, and so on.

15. See Vicuña's autobiography, "Performing Memory," included in this book.

16. "Vaso de leche" was performed in Colombia in 1979 to protest the contamination of milk with paint (in order to increase yield), which lead to the death of nearly 2000 children. Vicuña, in the autobiography included here, explains that this "action" was simultaneously taken with others in Chile, as part of CADA's (Colectivo de Acciones de Arte/ Art Actions Collective) work *Para No Morir De Hambre in el Arte* (To Not Die of Hunger in Art). Although Vicuña's participation is not recognized in her article, Nelly Richard explains that this collective work "diagnosed the wants of the national body by using the symbol of milk to denounce poverty, hunger, or other economic deprivations" (204).

17. See especially Fusco's introduction.

18. This poem was recorded by Franciscan missionary Bernandino de Sahagún in 1528. A translation into English by David Guss is included in *The Oxford Book of Latin American Poetry*, Eds.

Cecilia Vicuña and Ernesto Livón-Grosman (New York: Oxford University Press, 2009).

19. "But the hollow is soothing,/ we can lure it with a thread" (trans. Roberto Tejada). Lezama Lima's poem, "Pabellón del vacío" first appeared in *Fragmentos a su imán* (1978).

20. *Otoño*, Museo Nacional de Bellas Artes, Santiago, Chile, 1971.

21. Instrumental were Tedlock's *The Spoken Word and the Work of Interpretation*, especially "On the Translation of Style in Oral Narrative" (31-61), and "Phonography and the Problem of Time in Oral Narrative Events" (194-215); as well as Rothenberg's "Total Translation."

WORKS CITED ("PERFORMING MEMORY," "THE QUASARS," "LISTENING")

Roland Barthes. "Listening." *The Responsibility of Forms: Critical Essays on Music, Art, and Representation*. Trans. Richard Howard. Berkeley: U of California Press, 1991.

Cadogan, Leon. *AYVU RAPYTA: Textos Míticos de los Mbya-Guaraní del Guairá.* São Paulo, Brazil: USP, 1959.

Calvo, César. *Las tres mitades de Ino Moxo.* Iquito, Perú: Talleres Editorial Gráfica Labor, 1981.

——. *The Three Halves of Ino Moxo: Teachings of the Wizard of the Upper Amazon*, Trans. Kenneth Symington. Rochester, VT: Inner Traditions, Intl., 1995.

Chapman, Anne. *Drama and Power in a Hunting Society.* Cambridge: Cambridge UP, 1982.

——. *Selk'nam (Ona) Chants of Tierra del Fuego, Argentina.* Recorded by Chapman from March to June, 1966. Folkway Records: Ethnic Folkways Library (1972).

Classen, Constance. *Inca Cosmology and the Human Body.* Salt Lake City: U of UT Press, 1993.

Costa-Gavras, *Constantinos, dir. State of Siege.* Reggane Films, 1972. Film

Erickson, Clark L. "Raised Field Agriculture in the Lake Titicaca Basin: Putting Ancient Agriculture Back to Work." *Expedition* 30.1 (1988): 8-16.

García Gómez, Emilio, Ed. and Trans. *Poemas arábigoandaluces.* 1930. Buenos Aires: Espasa-Calpe, 1960.

Pellegrini, Aldo, Ed. *Antologia de la poesía surrealista de la lengua francesa*, Buenos Aires: Compañía General Fabril Editora, 1961

McKibben, Bill. *The End of Nature.* New York: Anchor Books, 1997.

——. "Nature Without People?" *New York Review of Books,* 46.1 (Aug 12, 1999): 2. Web. July 14, 2011.

Neruda, Pablo. *Confieso que he vivido.* Barcelona: Random House. 2003 (1974).

Piombino, Nick. "The Aural Ellipsis and the Nature of Listening in Contemporary Poetry." *Close Listening: Poetry and the Performed Word.* Ed. Charles Bernstein. New York: Oxford University Press, 1998. 53-72.

Sawyer, Alan R. *Ancient Andean Arts in the Collection of the Krannert Art Museum*. Urbana-Champaign: U of IL Press, 1975.

Sullivan, Lawrence. *Icanchu's Drum: An Orientation to Meaning in South American Religions*. NY: Macmillan, 1988.

Tedlock, Barbara. *Time and the Highland Maya*. Albuquerque: U of NM Press, 1982.

Tribu No. *El Corno Emplumado (The Plumed Horn)* 25 (Mexico, 1968).

— —. (Claudio Bertoni. Marcelo Charlín, Gonzalo Millán, Francisco Rivera, and Cecilia Vicuña). *Deliciosas criaturas perfumadas* (Santiago, no date/1970?).

Vicuña, Cecilia. "Carta a los Bosques Pellümawida." *Rattapallax 11/ Centenary of Pablo Neruda* (2004): 78-79.

— —. dir., author, and performer. *cloud-net*. Cinematography, Francesco Cincotta. Eds. Chris Borkowski and Paige Saez. 7:10 minutes. New York, NY, 1998. Video.

— —. *cloud-net* (exhibition catalog). New York: Art in General, 1999.

— —. *El Templo*. Trans. Rosa Alcalá. Art by Manel Lledós. NY: Situations Press, 2001.

— —."Fake Waterfall." Trans. R. Alcalá. *XCP: Cross Cultural Poetics. 8 / "Authenticating (Dis) Location / (Dis)Locating Authenticity"* (2001): 50-51.

— —. *Instan*. Berkeley: Kelsey St. Press, 2002.

— —."Libro Desierto / Desert Book." Trans. R. Alcalá. *A Book of the Book*. New York: Granary Books, 2000. 286-289.

— —. "Luis Gómez." Trans. R. Alcalá. *XCP: Cross Cultural Poetics* 8: 52-53.

— —. "Mother and Daughter." Trans. Suzanne Jill Levine. *American Poetry Review* 24.3: (1995): 19.

— —. "Mother of Pearl." Trans. R Alcalá. *Open City* 14 (Winter 2001-2002):153.

— —. *Saboramí*. England-Latin America: Beau Geste Press, 1973. N. pag.

— —. "Se Mi Ya / Seed Me Now, See You Later," Trans. Rosa Alcalá. *Rattapallax 9* (2003). CD.

— —. *Semi Ya* (art catalog). Santiago de Chile: Galería Gabriela Mistral, 2000.

— —. "Thread of the Voice." (Transcript by Kenneth Sherwood of a performance at SUNY Buffalo, 10 March 1994). *RIF/T: An Electronic Space for Poetry, Prose, and Poetics*. Eds. Kenneth Sherwood and Loss Pequeño Glazier (Spring 1995). <http://www.wings.buffalo.edu/epc/rift/rift04/vicu0401.html>

— —. "Transcript from a Performance at St. Mark's Poetry Project, May 15, 2002." *The Literary Review: Global New York*, 46.2 (2003): 325-329.

— —. *Unravelling Words & the Weaving of Water*. Trans. Eliot Weinberger and Suzanne Jill Levine. Saint Paul, MN: Graywolf Press, 1992.

CONTRIBUTOR BIOGRAPHIES

MARIA DAMON is the author of *The Dark End of the Street: Margins in American Vanguard Poetry and Postliterary "America": From Bagel Shop Jazz to Micropoetries*; co-author (with mIEKAL aND and Jukka-Pekka Kervinen) of several print and online books of poetry; and co-editor (with Ira Livingston) of *Poetry and Cultural Studies: A Reader.*

LINDA DUKE currently serves as director of the Marianna Kistler Beach Museum of Art at Kansas State University. She is perennially fascinated by the nature of thought, especially the relationship between language and non-verbal experience.

NADA GORDON is the author of *Folly*, *V. Imp*, *Are Not Our Lowing Heifers Sleeker than Night-Swollen Mushrooms?*, *foriegnn bodie*, *Swoon*, and *Scented Rushes*. Recently she has been thinking a lot about Burma, Star Trek, and all things baroque.

JENA OSMAN'S books of poetry include *Public Figures* (Wesleyan 2012) and *The Network* (Fence Books 2010). She co-edits the ChainLinks book series with Juliana Spahr. In 2011, ChainLinks reprinted Cecilia Vicuña's 1973 book *Saborami.*

KENNETH SHERWOOD is Associate Professor of English at Indiana University of Pennsylvania, where he teaches poetry, theory, and digital writing. His essay on the translation of Severo Sarduy is forthcoming in the *Shippensburg Journal of Modern Languages.*

JULIANA SPAHR is the author of several books, including *Well Then There Now* (Black Sparrow, 2011) and *That Winter The Wolf Came* (Commune Editions, 2015).

DENNIS TEDLOCK'S books include *Finding the Center: The Art of the Zuni Storyteller*; *Breath on the Mirror: Mythic Voices and Visions of the Living Maya*, *Days from a Dream Almanac*, *Rabinal Achi: A Mayan Drama of War and Sacrifice*, and *2000 Years of Mayan Literature*. He won the PEN Translation Prize for *Popol Vuh: The Mayan Book of the Dawn of Life*. Forthcoming is *An Archaeology of Architecture*. He teaches in the Poetics Program at the University at Buffalo.

EDWIN TORRES has work forthcoming in the anthologies, *Postmodern American Poetry Vol. 2* (Norton), *The Heath Anthology of American Literature, Vol. E 7th Edition* (Cenguage Learning), and *Kindergarde: Avant-garde Poems, Plays, Stories and Songs For Children.*

RODRIGO TOSCANO'S books include *Deck of Deeds* (Counterpath, 2012) and *Collapsible Poetics Theater*, a 2007 National Poetry Series Selection. His writing has appeared in the anthologies, *Against Expression*, *Diasporic Avant Gardes*, and *Best American Poetry*. He works for the Labor Institute out of a laptop, tethered to a Droid, residing in airports, occupying poetics in mid-flight.

COLOPHON

This third printing of *Spit Temple*, consisting of seven hundred and fifty copies, was printed on 100% recycled paper and bound at McNaughton & Gunn in Saline, Michigan. Covers for this printing were printed offset at Prestige Printing in Brooklyn, New York, with die cutting by Hodgins Engraving, Batavia, New York. Design and typesetting by goodutopian.

Ugly Duckling Presse is a nonprofit art and publishing collective devoted to the dissemination of new poetry, translations, lost works, performance texts, and books by artists. UDP favors emerging, international, and "forgotten" writers with well-defined formal or conceptual projects that are difficult to place at other presses; its full-length books, periodicals, and limited-edition works often contain handmade elements that call attention to the labor and history of bookmaking.

UDP's Dossier Series was founded in 2008 to expand the formal scope of the press. Dossier titles don't share a single genre or form—poetry, essay, criticism, interview, artist book—but an investigative impulse.

For more information on UDP, visit us on the web: www.uglyducklingpresse.org